The Gardener's World

The History, the Beauty, th

by Josephine von Miklos
and Evelyn Fiore.
Special photography
by Josephine von Miklos.

———

Foreword by Richard A. Howard,
director, Arnold Aboretum,
Harvard University

A Ridge Press Book

Riches of The Gardener's World

Random House, New York

Contents

1. *Miracles and Mysteries* page 10

2. *The Grand Designs* page 28

3. *The Elements* page 40

4. *Cycle of Life* page 58

5. *From the Wilderness: Woods and Waters* page 68

6. *From the Wilderness: Field and Meadow* page 94

*Published in the United States by
Random House, Inc., New York, and simultaneously in
Canada by Random House of Canada, Limited, Toronto.
Prepared and produced by The Ridge Press, Inc.
Library of Congress Catalog Card Number: 69-16173
Printed in Italy by Mondadori, Verona.
This edition distributed by
Crown Publishers, Inc.*

*Editor-in-Chief: Jerry Mason
Editor: Adolph Suehsdorf
Art Director: Albert Squillace
Associate Editor: Moira Duggan
Associate Editor: Barbara Hoffbeck
Art Associate: David Namias
Art Associate: Egbert Teague
Art Production: Doris Mullane*

7. Composing the Garden *page 112*

8. In Wild and Stony Ground *page 142*

9. By Still and Running Waters *page 164*

10. Plants and Life *page 178*

11. Cities in Flower *page 202*

12. World Within *page 216*

13. A Place for Meditation *page 232*

Foreword

This age of man's technological accomplishments reveals, also, his continued dependence on the growing plant. In his current understanding of how plants grow, he stands nearly as much in awe of the capabilities of nature as did his predecessors in civilizations past, who associated with mythical gods the beauty and the bounty of the flowering plant. Agriculture and horticulture, as sciences and practical arts, are today the derivatives of man's accumulation of experiences with the plant as a useful and a beautiful living organism. The search for sustenance in the variety of green plants has dominated the life of man on this earth and remains a foremost problem of our times. Yet, throughout his history, man has found time to admire what he may not thoroughly understand: the seasonal development and temporal variation of a seed into a plant which flowers and sets new seeds. Man has learned to use the plant in all parts of this cycle. Wherever he lives, he has found the spot where the plant grows best. He has taken plants with him as he travels and he has brought back plants from areas foreign to him—if they please him. An appreciation of usefulness and beauty characterize the way man has lived in a world of plants.

A few orders of social insects are known to cultivate plant materials for food; to garden solely for beauty is an attribute of man alone. Man may grow a single plant in the smallest room; maintain a window box of flowers or vegetables in a mountain of apartments; distinguish his rented plot of land with a personal planting; cultivate an estate of spacious vistas; or share the public gardens that his government has developed.

In all, the pleasure is individual and the personal search is for beauty.

Josephine von Miklos has recorded man's interest in plants throughout history and his use and associations with plants. She has retrieved the plans and reproduced the impressions of the great gardens of many ages. The scanty facts of the Hanging Gardens of Babylon, one of the seven wonders of the ancient world, contrast sharply with the vivid details of the outstanding gardens of recent and current times. A summary of how plants grow and how they vary in form leads to a discussion of where plants grow and how they are related to their environment; it culminates in practical suggestions for designing a garden you can enjoy. Throughout this book are the intriguing myths of the origin of plant names and uses, little-known facts about the characteristics of individual species, and, frequently, the role of individual botanists in the introduction of the plant to cultivation. The interpretations of flora by artists of lasting fame are offered in contrast with equally beautiful renditions by men whose names are forgotten, but whose admiration of a lovely scene or a beautiful plant remains. Mrs. von Miklos' contribution is that of an artist who records with her camera the vista, the intimate close image, and the magnified detail of the pattern or color of the whole plant, or a small part of it, and reveals with words of love an admiration of the growing, flowering plant.

This is a book to enjoy. May you treasure it and derive pleasure and knowledge from it, as have I.

Richard A. Howard

Director, Arnold Arboretum of Harvard University

Introduction

If you want to know how to dig a hole to plant a rose bush or a mountain laurel, when to put tulip bulbs into the ground, how to spread flower seeds so they will sprout and come into bloom, this is not your book. But if you want to find out what it means to tend a garden, what pleasures you share with millions of people all over the world, or why one plant has been sacred and another cursed, this is your book.

The world of the gardener and the lover of nature is, in fact, all worlds at all times. It is the world of pleasure, solace, and even reverence. It is the world of food, healthful and humble for everyday needs, or delicate and rare for the refined palates of gourmets. It is the world of healing and medicine, of hope and revival. And although no plant has yet been found which will give us eternal youth, a good many at least promise us beauty. For a tiny blossom in the deepest woods appears like a shining miracle in the darkness; the scent of a rose in the early morning prepares our day for the good things to come. And to be able to make a primrose bloom in midwinter imparts a sense of triumph shared only by poets.

So walk with us for a while—through the wilderness where all plants began, to the princely gardens where they bloomed. See how an Egyptian sculptor designed the lotus blossom which was to adorn the capital of a temple column, how a medieval monk tended his monastery's garden, how a great French garden designer made plants look like embroidery fit for a queen.

The work of this book could never have been accomplished without the generous help of many people. Elizabeth Burris-Meyer of New York and Pound Ridge put at my disposal her great knowledge of gardening, as well as her distinguished collection of ancient herbals; Theodora Hausman of Washington, D. C., collected research material from our nation's capital and helped on journeys of exploration. Help came from other friends and neighbors in Pound Ridge: Muriel Hinerfeld, who shared her vast horticultural knowledge; Katharine Getsinger, who designed the two lovely round gardens on pages 200 and 201; and Marjorie Newlon. I must also pay tribute to my late friend Lyndel Stone of Pound Ridge, who was the inspiration of countless gardeners and nature lovers, and who found the chart of perennials on pages 138 to 141 in an antique shop some years ago.

I must also thank Natalie Hays Hammond of North Salem, New York, who put her Japanese stroll garden at my disposal, and Helen Whitman and Charlotte Lee, who endured my countless attempts to photograph in their Toolshed Herb Nursery at North Salem, New York. I am grateful to the owners of the Brookside Nurseries of Darien, Connecticut, who allowed me to photograph in their gardens and hothouses.

I am deeply grateful to Gina and Helen Federico, Rees Mason, Margery Sachs, Anne and John Straus, all of Pound Ridge, and Alice Goodman of Stamford, Connecticut, for permission to photograph their gardens; and to the landscape architects Charles Middleleer of Darien, Connecticut, and James Fanning of Stamford, Connecticut, whose work I have admired for many years. Nor would the job of collecting the pictorial material ever have been accomplished without the help of Mrs. Catherine Struse-Springer of the Metropolitan Museum of Art, New York; Miss Louise Houllier of the Pierpont Morgan Library, New York; Miss Jean C. Hildreth of the Abby Aldrich Rockefeller Folk Art Collection, Williamsburg; and the Press Bureau of Colonial Williamsburg, Virginia; Dr. Erwin M. Auer of the Kunsthistorisches Museum, Vienna; and Mr. T. C. Mitchell of the Department of Western Asiatic Antiquities and his colleagues of the Department of Manuscripts of the British Museum. Finally, I should like to acknowledge the assistance of Evelyn Fiore in the writing of the text.

May this book stand as a small monument to all who revere nature and love its marvels.

Josephine von Miklos

Pound Ridge, New York

October, 1968

1. Miracles and Mysteries

Making a garden is an act of creation. It is man working with nature instead of against it, as he does in so many of his activities, imposing on life forces over which he otherwise has no control a form conceived by his taste, judgment, accumulated knowledge, and sensory responses.

The primary job, of course, is nature's. From the thin layer of fertile soil that covers the land regions of the earth, blooming and fruiting plants grow in their seasons, quite without man's help. Ferns and trees were fully evolved long before he made his appearance; even the flowers preceded him by about seventy-five million years.

This free, wild beauty would exist, as perhaps it did in the Garden of Eden, with or without man. What man has contributed is form. By his art and labor he composes these growing things into what we think of as gardens. His planned garden may be no more beautiful than a hillside blowing with wild flowers, but it is a more selective, more personal beauty, one he can perhaps more easily understand and enjoy. And it is his. It is a work of cooperation between him and nature, and to this extent he shares in nature's miracle. Perhaps this is why the backbreaking work of gardening is also such mysteriously satisfying and exciting work. It is surely why gardeners become more monomaniacal in devotion to their hobby than do cat lovers or bridge players. To dig into the earth, performing certain seemingly magical rites, and thus become at least partly responsible for the life that comes up from it is almost as marvelous to the twentieth-century gardener as it must have been to the primitive men who first perceived the relationship between seeds and roots in the ground and green life on the surface.

The earliest gardeners, of course, were neither artists nor hobbyists. They were simply farmers. Quite possibly the whole thing started when some enterprising Stone Age woman, whose mate turned out to be an inadequate hunter, experimented with the purple berries that grew around her cave in an effort to supplement her family's diet. If this incident had been recorded, it would have been the first historical example of victory being snatched from the jaws of defeat. For having discovered that much of the vegetation around them was edible, men proceeded purposely to grow it, thus advancing themselves to a new evolutionary plateau. They became agriculturists.

By an even more obscure process, they learned of the medicinal and curative powers of plants, and also of their deadly poisons.

From an anthropological point of view, agriculture is a prerequisite to civilization. The moment primitive tribesmen learn that

they no longer have to chase all of their food, but rather that after doing some preliminary groundwork they can sit still and have crops come up in predictable places and even quantities, they are on their way to developing a stable social situation. Members stake out a patch of private property, edge it with brambles to keep out wolves and possibly their less industrious neighbors, and gradually find that they are accumulating leisure to develop talents with which they can do more than merely sustain life. Along with other arts and crafts, pleasure gardens became an indicator of a civilization's sophistication. Every civilization that has made an enduring mark on history—in every era, from China, to India, to Persia, and the West—has left a record of its gardens.

But even as man learned to farm, thus controlling to some extent the miracle of life, it seemed to him no less miraculous. When Captain James Cook landed in New Zealand in 1769, he found planted around the huts of the Stone Age Maoris the vine we now call clianthus. It was not eaten; it was nurtured only because it was pretty and because it was alive. It must have been very early indeed in man's history that he realized that, beyond his physical need for what the earth produces, he must also remain in touch with the inexplicable power of life that thrusts from the soil. To be reminded that withering and apparent death could be followed by a mysterious resurgence gave him hope that his own fate was not irrevocable. If the plant that appeared to die was in reality only dormant, why should not the end of a man be only the preliminary to a new beginning?

Early religions developed around this mystery of renewal. Trees, particularly,

were venerated. The powerful roots, the persistent vigor of life flowing through the trunk, the incredible rebirth from branches that appeared quite dead all convinced early man that the tree was a magic or holy symbol of his own progress through the universe. Tree worship sprang up independently in every inhabited region of the world. From the clouded beginnings of life in the North comes the Norse tradition of the sacred ash Yggdrasill, from which the first man was believed to have sprung. Yggdrasill's three roots go down into death, or hell, into the realm of the giants where wisdom dwells, and into Asgard where the gods and fates hold court.

To hurt or destroy certain trees was a criminal offense in some societies. In the belief that trees could heal, the sick were often dragged through the divided trunk of a hollow tree. The ribbon- and flower-decked Maypole, still danced around in the springtime where there are peasants old enough to remember the tradition, is a survival of an ancient fertility rite in which a young tree was planted outside a girl's room to ensure her fruitfulness. Less romantically, it was sometimes planted before the stables; it was important for people tied to the land that their animals reproduce, too.

This identification of man's existence and well-being with trees appears in all mythologies. One of the regeneration myths of the Egyptian god Osiris (identified with Tammuz in Babylonia, and Adonis in Phoenicia) tells that he died each year; his body then floated upon the sea to Byblos on the Phoenician coast, where he was reincarnated as a young tree. Also from Egypt comes the three-thousand-year-old "Tale of the Two Brothers" in which a man having given his

13

heart to an acacia dies when it is cut down.

The symbolic Tree of Life recurs in every Eastern religion, and persists to the present day as a decorative motif. Until the Hebrews were forbidden such fetishes, cedars and palms had special significance for them. The bo tree, a wild fig, was sacred in parts of the East. Longevity alone makes some trees impressive. In Ceylon there is a bo tree whose life, local legend claims, can be traced back to a parent tree that existed in 245 B.C. The redwoods of California and Oregon are credited with ages of four hundred to two thousand years. Man cannot help being awed by this staggering span of years when he himself hardly dares to hope for more than the Biblical three score and ten.

These two aspects of man's relationship to plants—that they provided food and a possible key to the secret of his own existence—were well-developed by the time of the first civilization of which we have adequate records. This was the powerful kingdom of Sumer, which flourished more than three thousand years B.C., in spite of recurrent and devastating floods, in the fertile but unstable delta formed by the Tigris and Euphrates rivers in Mesopotamia.

Because the Sumerians invented a consistent system of cuneiform writing, and kept records on clay tablets baked so hard that a surprising number of their fragments have been recovered, we know that among their achievements was an effective irrigation system that fed a variety of crops—barley, onions and other vegetables, and extensive date orchards. Their first houses were made of woven reeds and values were measured in barley before they used gold and silver as mediums of exchange. Their temples were set in sacred groves which grew not only food but medicinal plants of which the priests made knowledgeable use.

Sargon I, powerful ruler of Akkad and conqueror of Sumer, left records describing himself as a gardener. In a legend that predates the story of Moses, he relates that as an infant he was placed in a reed basket and set adrift upon a river. The river bore him to Akki, "the irrigator," who reared and cherished him and trained him as a gardener. Sargon continues: "My service...was pleasing to Istar [originally a goddess of fertility; later, it appears, a generic name for all goddesses] and I became King."

Flowers were important to the Sumerians; their clay tablets show that they were used in decoration, in ceremony, in ritual headdresses. But whether the Sumerians were interested in nonutilitarian gardens we do not know.

The Near Eastern civilizations that succeeded the Akkadian, the Assyrian and the Babylonian, also left little evidence of garden areas. In their crowded urban centers anyone who craved greenery probably had to grow his plants on a rooftop, and he had to be wealthy to do that. Trees were highly prized, and brought back as trophies by rulers—from Tiglath-pileser, in the second millennium B.C., to Sennacherib, in the first—from their conquests abroad. Great parks surrounded the oriental magnificence of the royal residences; acres of these were maintained as hunting preserves, but other areas, dotted with pavilions to shelter outdoor dining and other diversions, evidently were used as pleasure grounds.

A bas-relief in the British Museum shows the Assyrian king Ashurbanipal enjoying an outdoor victory feast in 660 B.C. As he dines and drinks, listens to music, and ad-

14

mires his wife, he can also refresh himself with occasional glances at the severed head of his enemy, which hangs on a tree nearby. Ashurbanipal's interests, however, were not entirely barbaric. From his enormous library come cuneiform texts that contain all kinds of information, much of it about plants and plant uses. Perfumes and incense, which had been known even in earlier times, were familiar commodities to the Assyrians. Originally they appear to have been associated with purification and ritual cleansing; the fragrances were meant to make the wor-

shiper acceptable to the gods. By the time of Ashurbanipal—and certainly among contemporary Egyptians—they were being used to make the wearers more acceptable to each other. Some of the oils and scents may also have helped protect the skin from the heat and insects of the area. From Ashurbanipal's records we learn that oils were extracted from almond, castor, lettuce, olive, radish, safflower, and sesame plants. Natural perfumes were distilled from bitter almond, aniseed, cedar, cinnamon, citron, ginger, heliotrope, mimosa, peppermint, rose, rose-

Wall painting of 1250 B.C. represents house and garden of Apuy, a Theban sculptor

15

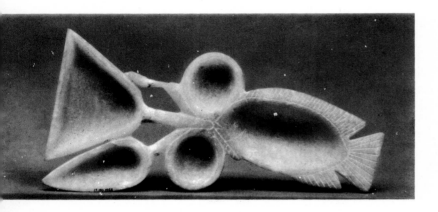

Seven ziggurats, mimicking the utilitarian planting of terraced hillsides, ascended in layers of diminishing size, symbolizing the link between earth and heaven in the same way as the Tower of Babel was supposed to have done. Each layer was heavily planted, the flat top most lavishly of all to provide an outdoor room from which royalty could view the countryside. The terraces were supported by hollow pillars filled with soil, so that trees planted above them could take root, and the arched areas beneath the terraces, we are told, contained "many stately rooms...for all purposes."

The civilization of Egypt was likewise heightened by the advantages of a riverside location. Without the Nile, it is probable that the area the Greeks eventually named Egypt would never have achieved its eminence in the ancient world. In fact, it was called "the gift of the Nile," by the Greek historian Herodotus. The river's recurrent floods left in their wake enormously fertile soil which the Egyptians learned to use to advantage, developing the first hydraulic engineering system and canals to divert

Lotus form appears in alabaster dish of ancient Egypt (above) and sketch for capitals of Theban columns (below). Slab fragment (opposite) has carved Assyrian lions lazing in royal park.

mary, and sandalwood.

Though Assyria and Babylonia were enemies, geographical and historical circumstances must have made their ways of life very similar. Grains, dates, and olives (which had been imported and then cultivated) were important trade items—so much so that a favorite military maneuver of an invading army was to destroy the enemy's olive groves. Assyrians and Babylonians farmed, rather than gardened.

Yet, paradoxically, one of the great gardens of all time, one of the seven wonders of the world, is thought to have enriched Babylon about 550 B.C.: the Hanging Gardens, created by Nebuchadnezzar, according to legend, to comfort a Median wife longing for the green mountains of her homeland. No contemporary descriptions exist, but word-of-mouth reports of the gardens, finally written down in the first century B.C. by the Greek historians Strabo and Diodorus, are so elaborate and detailed that it seems carping to doubt their basic facts. The terraced construction they describe was typical of the farming techniques of the region. According to them, the gardens covered many acres, and really appear to have been more an auxiliary palace or state building than a garden in our terms.

overflow to arid land areas. On this fertile land they grew a variety of crops for consumption and trade: beans, cabbage, melons, radishes, lettuce, flax, dates, figs, bananas, and pomegranates, among others.

On the wall of a tomb in Thebes is preserved a notable painting of the elaborate garden of an official of Amenhotep III, so carefully detailed that it offers practically a review of Egyptian garden practices of the period around 1400 B.C. Like other records, it indicates that the Egyptians designed geometrical, formal gardens, reflecting a taste for ordered luxury and a ceremonious social and religious life. The gardens were walled and divided by avenues of trees. Grapes grew over tall arbors that already resembled our modern pergolas, and fruit trees and vivid masses of poppies, irises, and cornflowers grew in checkerboard-style beds. Roses, sacred to the goddess Isis, were grown in special enclaves, and although Greece and

Rome cultivated their own rose gardens, Egypt grew roses in such abundance that it became, in a later era, the ancient world's chief source of supply. The rose petals which carpeted the floors and tables at any properly arranged Roman banquet came by the shipload from Egypt.

Trees were planted formally around another feature that distinguished any Egyptian garden large enough to be used for pleasure: water. Pools, even small lakes were the delight of those gardeners who could afford them. Sometimes, as in the Theban garden, ducks and lotus floated on them; sometimes they were used for bathing. Amenhotep III possessed a "pond" said to have been a mile long and a thousand feet wide which may have been used for boating.

Like the lotus and the date palm—which appear over and over as stylized motifs on columns and artifacts—the papyrus plant, now virtually extinct, was grown through-

17

18

out the delta region. Weedlike and tufted with nondescript green-white umbels, it added nothing in the way of beauty, but its myriad uses made it almost fundamental to Egyptian economy. Its long, thick rhizomes were used not only for food but for fuel and for making a variety of everyday utensils; the pith of the stem also was eaten; from the woody exterior came boats, sails, ropes; and, of greater historical importance than any other of its products, from the stems came the writing material the Egyptians manufactured.

What is interesting from a gardener's point of view is that around 1170 B.C., when Egypt had already begun to decline, Ramses III enlarged the gardens and orchards of On (Heliopolis), so that more men might enjoy them. It appears that the rulers of ancient Egypt understood that beauty is an essential of a civilized life, and took pride in their ability to create it.

The classic Greeks, who rose as Egypt declined, and the early Persians, whom they eventually defeated, contributed little to garden design or philosophy. The Greeks lived in a harsh, mountainous land where only vines and the olive tree grew well; farms outside the cities supplied the increasingly urban civilization with food and flowers for garlands. Pot gardening was popular in Athens, and in midsummer rooftops were bright with Gardens of Adonis which symbolized the god's death and resurrection. When there was space for a garden, it was likely to be put behind the house, protected from the busy street and bordered by high banks or trees that made it a sort of garden room. The beds were planted with lilies, violets, roses, hyacinths, and were often decorated with statues.

We cannot be sure that Homer's description of the garden of Alcinous is accurate but, at the very least, it must surely describe the kinds of things that were grown in Greece about 700 B.C.:

Outside the palace yard,
    stretching out
From the gates, lies a fine four-
    acre orchard, with a hedge
On either side. Here tall trees
    are thriving,
Heavy with pears and pomegranates,
    with glossy apples,
Sweet figs and luscious plump
    olives. Year round, winter
Or summer, their fruit never fails,
    but here is always
Fruit for the West Wind's breath
    to quicken and ripen,
Pear upon pear, apple on apple,
    cluster
On cluster of grapes, and fig upon
    fig . . .

As Athens grew into the center of Greek civilization, its bare open squares were planted with trees that gradually transformed some of them into public parks. These grew so crowded, and were so hard to maintain because of the meager water supply, that the schools of philosophy were moved outside the city proper. The academy in which Plato taught, in the valley of the Kephissos, became a well-watered grove with trim avenues bordered by plane trees and narrow, shaded "philosophers' walks." Aristotle and Socrates taught at the Lyceum in a splendid grove north of the city. The schools eventually became so popular that some of the philosophers moved again into schools and gardens of their own. Epicurus,

Top: Greek women gather apples on red-figured krater of c. 460 B.C. Far left: Physician prepares cough medicine on page of 13th-century Dioscorides manuscript. Left: Olive tree in modern Israel.

the first to do so, was said to have spent seven thousand drachmas laying out his garden (a drachma was a day's wage). Pliny may have been upset by this when he wrote, somewhat waspishly, "... up to his [Epicurus'] time it had never been thought of to dwell in the country in the middle of town."

When Aristotle died, his pupil Theophrastus inherited his library and his teaching mantle in the Lyceum, and later laid the foundations of the science of botany. He recorded for the first time the botanical knowledge accumulated during the preced-

ing millenniums, and in *History of Plants* and *Causes of Plants* he discusses more than four hundred plants. His observations influenced students to the time of the Renaissance.

While the Greeks were laying the groundwork of scientific thinking, their physical world was still strangely primitive, alive with major and minor deities. Sacred groves enclosed the temples of the important gods. There was hardly a plant that did not have its associated spirit. We inherit countless myths of the dryads and hamadryads who inhabited trees. The pine was sacred to Pan,

20

the oak to Zeus, the olive to Athena. Daphne, fleeing from Apollo, became the laurel. Even Aristotle's logical, methodized approach to natural science allowed him to believe that trees had passions, perception, and reason; it is easy to see how the ordinary Greek lived side by side with the deities in such intimate contact that it was sometimes permitted a mortal to marry one.

The Greeks were fond of roses, and many myths collected about this symbol of beauty and love. Sacred to Aphrodite, it was inherited by her son Eros, who broadened its significance in an unexpected direction. With his mother's amorous indiscretions in mind, Eros presented the rose to Harpocrates, god of silence, to persuade him to conceal the follies of the other gods. When the Romans adopted the Greek pantheon the rose remained sacred to beauty and love —Venus and Cupid—but became as well the symbol of discretion. When important state affairs were to be discussed in secret, a rose was hung from the ceiling of the council chamber, making the conference—in a term familiar to this day—*sub rosa*.

The earliest Romans farmed in order to eat, and sold their surplus in the city markets to urbanites who had only enough space for the Roman version of window-box gardening. But as Rome grew, so did its wealthy classes of merchants, nobles, and politicians.

In A.D. 62, Pliny the Younger could divide his time between a town house and two country places, one on the sea at Ostia and one at Tusci, where he—and the labor of some of his five hundred slaves—maintained an elaborate pleasure garden that seems to have had little to do with agriculture. Pliny's garden sloped down from a

terrace into a variety of landscaped areas. Box hedges divided the sections and outlined paths. Acanthus was used as a ground cover; fountains, statues, and marble garden furniture were set among the shrubs and flower beds. The box was clipped into many fanciful shapes; this practice, called topiary, originated with the Egyptians and was favored also by the Greeks.

The *Natural History* of Pliny's uncle, Pliny the Elder, describes the great variety of trees, plants, and shrubs in Roman gardens. Exotic plants and out-of-season flowers were grown in the first hothouses of which we have record, whose windows were made of thinly sliced mica or talc.

As Rome and its suburbs spread, Romans went farther afield into towns like Pompeii and Herculaneum. The ruins at Pompeii show essentially Greek houses on which the Romans imposed minor changes. Generally the garden area of a Pompeian house was at the back, in the peristyle or colonnaded courtyard, enclosed on one side by the house and on the others by walls or roofed walks, but with the center open to the sky. These courts, even when small, were beautifully landscaped with ivy-edged beds set with violets, roses, anemones, small fruit trees, statuary, and fountains fed by complicated water systems.

As Rome's upper classes took over more and more of the city, efforts were made to propitiate the crowded poor by the creation of public play areas and parks—the tombs of Augustus and Hadrian were surrounded with gardens open to the public; Caesar left his garden and game area to the populace; and Pompey added parks. Temple groves, cemeteries, and baths were all set within gardens to which the people had free access.

21

Knowledge of plants, the art of landscaping, and the engineering skill to maintain it transformed Rome into a true city of gardens. When Alaric the Goth marched into it in A.D. 408 there were at least seventeen hundred and eighty gardens waiting—with all of the rest of Rome—to be destroyed.

In the centuries that followed, western man struggled to hold on to the fundamentals of his civilization. Like other pleasures, gardening became irrelevant; it was hard enough for the ordinary man, at the mercy of pillaging armies and marauders, to farm enough for his own food supply.

But there were, as there had been for generations, magnificent gardens in the Orient. During the next few centuries, as the conquering Moorish armies moved westward, they spread across North Africa and into Spain the artful combinations of color, shade, water, and brilliant tile-work that had made Persian gardens into approximations of the paradise that, according to the Koran, would eventually receive the faithful. Many of the flowers that later, through the crusades and travelers, found their way into European gardens had already been developed by the Persians. In fact, those devoted gardeners found it so hard to go through their long, barren winters deprived of flowers that they transferred their beauty to the richly patterned rugs that have endured as an art form as well as an industry.

In most of Europe, during those lawless, war-harried years, monasteries were the shelters of peace and productivity and the guardians of knowledge. Gardening was part of the daily routine, as it is in many orders still. It was logical that the men of God should be the custodians of the fruits of the earth and the knowledge of how to

Opposite: Van der Weyden's "Annunciation" symbolizes purity of Virgin with traditional Madonna lily. Above: 15th-century French depiction of Susanna and the Elders in garden.

improve them, and that they should carry on the tradition of the priest-healers in their often extensive medicinal herbariums.

Guided by rules laid down by St. Benedict, members of the Benedictine monastery founded in 529 at Monte Cassino in Italy followed a daily pattern later imitated by other orders (and followed even today) in which self-sufficiency was all-important. Farming supplied the monastery table with vegetables, fruits, and bread; wines and liqueurs were made by secret formulas that are still cherished. The monks also acted as a sort of agricultural advisory service to local farmers, who had neither the time nor the resources to improve crops on their own.

St. Gallen, beside Lake Constance, was

23

Two walled gardens, one heavenly, one mundane, both 15th-century. "Little Paradise" (below) is by von Tieffenthal. Castle garden (opposite) is from French horticultural treatise.

another active agricultural center. Its garden plan shows that the orchard and kitchen gardens were the most important sections. But monks did grow flowers—sometimes even when their order did not sanction it—and one Scottish monastery came into dire disfavor with its paternal house when it was reported that, among other excesses, each monk had a pleasure garden of his own.

St. Gallen had no such restrictions. Out of it, in the ninth century, came the first medieval garden book. It was written by Walafrid Strabo, a monk to whom we also are indebted for the first biography of Charlemagne; and as he chronicles his love for the soil, his triumphs over weeds and frustrations over plants that will not flourish,

he might be any gardener before or since. The gardener, he advises, must be "full of zeal"; he must water seedlings tenderly with drops from the fingers, for a full stream from the water pot would be too rough. And for the matted roots of nettles that choked his beds, Strabo showed no Christian tolerance. He tore them up and rent them with his "tooth of Satan"—and there is no record that he ever felt apologetic for this attack upon what, after all, was simply another of God's products.

No matter how much pleasure Strabo found in his kitchen garden, he was on safe ground because it was clearly necessary to St. Gallen's welfare, but one wonders how he escaped censure when it came to his

cherished lilies and roses, for he writes of them in terms of undisguised response to their beauty. Of course, he throws in a careful reference to the symbolism which by that time the church had assigned to them—the lily sacred to the Virgin, the rose to the blood of the martyrs. But when he writes "Better and sweeter are they than all other plants . . ." Strabo is surely kneeling to loosen the dirt around their roots, drinking in scent and color, not worrying about symbolism at all.

The agriculturist-physician monk was active even in geographically isolated England, though abbots wrote to their brothers on the continent complaining that it was hard to keep pace with the latest developments in herbal medicine. The backbone of a monastery's medical library was still the classical Greeks and Romans, such as Theophrastus, and Pliny the Younger, augmented by the later medical treatises of the physicians Galen and Dioscorides. Many followers had added to the store of knowledge, and the monks themselves constituted an active information service as they traveled from house to house with plants and advice. By the tenth century English monks were also using the *Leech Book of Bald*, a Saxon doctor's manual probably compiled from information dating back to earlier times.

English soil and climate, which produce splendid gardens today, were working their magic in those earlier times also, and monks

*Top: Renaissance
conception of landscaping
for Roman tomb
of Emperor Augustus.
Above: 16th-century
watering cans.
Right: Elaborate Indian
palace garden is
from Annals of Akbar.*

permitted to grow flowers could have them in abundance and variety. Roses were indigenous; the white rose had been symbolic of England long before it became the House of York's emblem in the fifteenth-century Wars of the Roses. In the first century, Pliny the Younger could not decide whether the "isle of Albion" had been named for the white cliffs of Dover or for the masses of white roses the Romans found there. Among other flowers, monastery gardens grew lilies, irises, and poppies; peonies were used in cooking—as indeed were roses and violets—and their seeds as a charm against evil, though the churchmen could hardly have sanctioned this pagan throwback.

The castle of the early Middle Ages was a fortress, generally walled in upon itself on inaccessible ground, with warfare and defense its chief preoccupations and little space for gardens. But there had to be an area, however small, for the herbs from which the lady of the castle brewed her simples and possets, flavorings, dyes, and scents. "Family" doctoring—which in those days was likely to include lance and arrow wounds as well as toothaches—was almost entirely the responsibility of the chatelaine, who usually had been schooled by monks or nuns to considerable adeptness. If, in the stillroom where she worked with her herbs, she brewed an occasional love potion, or even poison, she probably did not discuss it with her clerical mentor.

As life grew safer, these small gardens expanded, sometimes even beyond the castle walls. Exotic ideas and additions returned with the crusaders: pavilions for shelter and outdoor games, caged singing birds, arched trellises under which lovers could meet in seclusion. Far Eastern flowers and trees sprang up in European gardens: Carnations, jasmine, hollyhocks, pomegranate and lemon trees, and the cedar of Lebanon were imported and thrived.

Tapestries and the exquisitely painted miniatures of the later Middle Ages leave no doubt that, while its gardens were partly dedicated to food and herb production, they were also designed for every kind of pleasure. The church, of course, was still in control; and so in the essentially religious Book of Hours the magnificent floral details are crowded with religious significance. The Virgin is surrounded by lilies; the Child plays with an iris, traditionally associated with royalty; near him is a sprouting vine, in accordance with Isaiah's prophecy: "There shall come a rod out of the stem of Jesse." Yet what we see is a garden whose sensuous delights can be appreciated by the most irreligious. From paintings and documents of the time we know that even in the unwelcoming English climate opportunity was made for outdoor games and dining. As the mistress of the castle went about her chores, she might pause to watch a game of draughts, or take care not to see one of her ladies dallying with a young squire on a half-hidden bench. The grass, studded with buttercups and daisies—the "day's eye" or "eye of God"—was often "daunced upon"; the tough little wildflowers could be counted on to spring up again as durably as they sprang up in the fields beyond.

Life was growing less threatening and mysterious; people went a little less in fear of their lives, and as a consequence were a little easier about enjoying themselves. In spite of the church, they were no longer so certain that pleasure in this life inevitably meant pain in the life to come.

In Italy, as the Middle Ages emerged brilliantly into the Renaissance, a wealthy middle class joined the nobility in developing a luxurious way of life in which all the arts were involved. Country life, as in the days of ancient Rome, became fashionable; patterns for it were found in Pliny's letters and in the *villa rustica* of the Roman past. Estate and palace gardens became awesomely magnificent. Formed around vast squares or rectangles, divided by straight rows of plantings or stonework, and decorated with pergolas, summerhouses, and columns, everything about the gardens was balanced, orderly, neoclassic. From the archeologically rich Italian ground old statues were excavated and mounted as focal points for sweeping vistas. Though they appreciated these legacies from the past, Florentines did not hesitate to break them and recombine the fragments into new "antiques" that better suited a whim of the moment or the needs of a particular spot. These gardens were glamorized with fountains and cascading water and evergreen plants clipped into elaborate topiary shapes that again reverted to the old Roman style. The landowner whose name was spelled out in box possessed the ultimate in status.

Many important gardens derived from the Florentine architect Alberti, who in the course of designing palaces for Cosimo de' Medici became the first modern landscape designer as well. Setting down his principles in *De re aedificatoria*, Alberti decreed that the main lines must be kept "in strict proportion and regularity, in case the pleasing harmony of the whole be lost in the attraction of individual plants." Yet the Renaissance Italians were sensitive to the "attraction of individual plants"—especially to the shape, scent, and color of flowers, which had lost most of their religious significance and now spoke joyously of sensuous beauty and earthly love. It is perhaps not a coincidence that the lush bloom not permitted to riot in gardens burst out lavishly in design. Carved and painted inlaid flowers appeared on fountains, vases, and in paintings and mosaics.

Even in the later Renaissance gardens, where baroque curves and lushness softened the classical austerity, artificiality still was imposed on nature. Elaborate, park-like villas like the Villa d'Este at Tivoli and the Borghese gardens of Rome could not really be imitated in other climates and therefore remained an Italian specialty. But the Villa d'Este's outdoor theater, created of turf and topiary, certainly inspired outdoor entertainment areas in France and England. Italy in this period also provided impetus to the spread of botanical gardens, most of them "physick" gardens attached to universities where medicine and botany were often taught by the same professor. These became progressively less medically oriented. By the time America got its first public botanical garden in 1731 in Philadelphia, its function was to serve the curiosity, pleasure, and education of anyone interested in plants.

While the Italians were manipulating nature into greater opulence, the French—equally unwilling to give it its head—turned their backs on rich baroque garden design and went by a totally different aesthetic route to obtain their own artificial effects. When André Le Nôtre created Versailles for Louis XIV, the prevailing spirit in France was that man was, or must aspire to be, a rational creature. The philosopher Pascal wrote,

"Man is made for thinking" and the ideal was a life controlled by pure logic, order, and reason. Even in his pleasures man must not be diverted by prettiness; Versailles had a minimum of flowers and no "informal" flower beds. (In addition, it was Le Nôtre's quirk that he heartily disliked flowers!) While it is now only a fraction of what it was when Louis delighted in showing it to foreign visitors, the grandeur of the design is still apparent—a design that took almost twenty years and astonishing feats of engineering and transportation to complete. Enormous trees were hauled from Flanders and Normandy. A series of canals was dug to bring water from Savoy to supply fourteen hundred water jets, of which only about six hundred remain. There was an enormous number of ponds and lakes, including some large enough for boating. It was a sublime park in the grandest manner possible, constructed and maintained at incalculable cost.

Le Nôtre also redesigned the Tuileries, which had been a loose arrangement of walks, park areas, and menageries, and in so doing planted the stately avenue of trees that became the Champs Elysées. Through his students, his influence spread across Europe, even as far as Russia. Nine years after his death in 1700 his disciple, Alexandre LeBlond, set forth his own version of the principles that had, in effect, purified and restored to elegance the last years of Renaissance garden design. He said that gardens should not be overhung, but should preserve plenty of open spaces, and be made to look bigger than they actually were by visual barriers such as hedges and balustrades. He laid down mathematical formulas: The length should be one and a half times the width; there should be three steps down from the house to the main walk, which should cross the garden from end to end. In particular, even the smallest garden must have about it "nothing mean," but carry an air of nobility and magnificence. LeBlond was not interested in designing cottage gardens for Everyman.

While Le Nôtre's influence brushed over Holland, great perspectives and sweeping vistas could have little meaning in a country where there was little land and less variety of terrain. A few Dutch gardeners responded over-enthusiastically to LeBlond's mathematical formulas and created stiff little gardens where the beds were not only of precise size and shape, but planted in the same manner—three tall flowers at the back, flanked by a low plant at either side, and so on—thus reinforcing the Dutch reputation for methodicalness.

Holland's importance to farming and gardening was in another area. Because the Dutch had struggled for every foot of arable land, reclaiming much of it from the encroaching seas, they had become the best farmers and flower growers in Europe. They worked their land intensively, with all the scientific knowledge available; great botanical gardens at Leyden and Groningen disseminated information throughout Europe; and Dutch adventuring along the eastern trade routes brought hundreds of new species to Europe. In the sixteenth century, Charles L'Ecluse, a professor at the University of Leyden, listed more than six hundred of these exotics in his history of rare plants.

Eventually this expertise blossomed in the New World. Dutch *bouwerij*, farms, flourished on Long Island soil that was very much like the Netherlanders' water-bound homeland. Early visitors to New Amsterdam re-

ported that, besides the inevitable tulips, the colonists were growing many kinds of roses, gillyflowers, eglantine (a sweetbriar rose), anemones, and even the clove tree, most of which had not appeared in America until the Dutch brought them over.

Le Nôtre's "grand manner" reached England early in the seventeenth century where it had to contend with the earlier, cozier style that even the wealthy British preferred: small gardens bursting with flowers of almost infinite variety, walled for privacy, and often retaining in the old castle style, hedges or interior walls to keep orchards, herbs, and flowers in separate sections. James I, like the Stuarts who came after him, was actively interested in gardening. He encouraged the formation of a guild to curtail sharp practices (like the sale of dead trees and rotten seeds that had become scandalously widespread) and to make sure that every so-called gardener was entitled by apprenticeship and license to practice the "mystery of gardening."

One of the great herbals of the time, *Para-*

disi in Sole Paradisus Terrestris, was produced by James' herbalist, John Parkinson, in 1629. Parkinson was a practical and practicing gardener, but like all of the monastic herbals from which his work descended—indeed, like the renowned *Herball* of John Gerard, which preceded it by about thirty years—*Paradisi in Sole* contains a mixed bag of plant lore: down-to-earth plant advice, a good deal of "physick" recipes for cosmetics as well as puddings, and an assortment of unreliable "information." Yet Parkinson was a comparatively sound man for his time.

This was a lively period in English gardening, for hundreds of previously unknown New World plants were coming across the Atlantic in exchange for many that were being sent by English gardeners to the colonies. Many foreign plants went into the great physic gardens at Chelsea and Oxford for study and use in medicine. The Tradescant family, gardeners to many nobles and later to Charles I, were famous contributors to this mutual enrichment. The elder John

Tradescant set the pattern by voyaging as far as the Barbary Coast, braving pirates and other dangers to bring back exotics that now flourish in great gardens like those of Hatfield House, which he designed for the Cecil family. His son John brought back from travels in Virginia the red maple, the American plane, and other newcomers, a few of which—the Michaelmas daisy, *Aster tradescanti*, is one—perpetuate the family name with a little of the glory it deserves.

Many handsome estate gardens were founded during this century, and people not lucky enough to possess such luxury could disport themselves in the new public gardens that grew up in and around London: Mulberry Gardens, the old Spring Garden near Charing Cross, Vauxhall (which began as Falkes' Hall), and Tatnum's at Tottenham Court, where thoughtful arrangements of shrubbery ensured privacy for dancing, gaming, and other diversions. As we know from the gossipy diary of Samuel Pepys, these were enormously popular until rowdy street gangs made them dangerous.

From Pepys up and down, it would almost appear that no Englishman could live through the seventeenth century without keeping a diary, and fortunately many of them were gardeners. One of the most notable was John Evelyn. Coming by marriage into possession of Sayes Court at Deptford, he gradually turned it into a showplace, combining the charm of Italian, French, and the old, heavily planted Tudor styles into a whole that he felt suited the nature of the grounds. Evelyn was also a crusading conservationist; *Sylva*, his book on trees, was a concerned plea for the protection of England's forests. It must have been traumatic for him when Peter the Great of Russia, to whom Sayes Court was briefly sublet, found eccentric pleasure in having himself carted through its magnificent hedges in a wheelbarrow—where no paths existed.

As the eighteenth century progressed into what is generally called the Age of Reason, all the arts were increasingly dominated by this ordered, almost mathematically symmetrical style.

Pleasure garden of Marie Antoinette's Petit Trianon.

33

Symmetry and perfect proportion were one thing, but the ruthless reshaping of nature into rigid green geometry was another, and even as the fashion prevailed English taste began to rebel against it. In 1712 Joseph Addison complained in the *Spectator* that British gardeners were distorting nature. "Our trees rise in Cones, Globes and Pyramids...I would rather look upon a tree in all its Luxuriancy and Diffusion ... than when it is thus cut and trimmed into a Mathematical Figure...."

At the same time, Alexander Pope turned his caustic pen against the ludicrous extremes of topiary work, and the influential Earl of Shaftesbury who, like Addison, had been excited by travel through the dramatic Roman campagna, wrote eloquently in praise of wild, natural beauty. All over England, garden walls came down. Hedges were moved so that there was no demarcation where the manor grounds ended and the free country began. Gloomy grottoes, wild jutting rocks, and streams that rambled ec-

centrically and vanished into the misty distance softened and enriched the English landscape. Unfortunately, where there was no grotto, one was contrived. Nonfunctional oriental drum bridges went from nowhere to nowhere across many a stream, like the famous one at Ken Wood in Highgate which is actually only a one-dimensional false front. Pointless temples and artificial "ruins" became indispensable. In Kensington Gardens, the designer William Kent even planted dead trees for dramatic contrast, and when criticized retorted that his aim was not to copy nature, but to improve it.

In the vanguard of the "naturalistic" or "landscape" gardening movement was Kent's apprentice and successor, Lancelot Brown, so remarkably able and prolific that he was far better known by his nickname, "Capability"—especially to the segment of England that could afford him. Brown swept over many of the fine old formal gardens with a ruthless hand, destroying much that was elegantly beautiful in his conviction that nothing was right unless it met his picturesque, romantic standards. By 1750 he was gardener to George II and responsible for Blenheim, Kew, and the gardens of more than a hundred other "stately homes" throughout England. Much of his work was altered in the nineteenth century when new plants—rhododendrons, the tulip tree, and other American imports—changed his effects. His work can be seen at Stowe in Buckinghamshire, now a boys' school, but in the mid-eighteenth century the vast, renowned showplace of Lord Cobham for whom Brown originally worked as a kitchen gardener.

The so-called landscape school was part of the already stirring rebellion against clas-

Theater and formal gardens —each with fountain—of Villa Mondragone in Frascati, near Rome.

34

sical order in all the arts, but that did not prevent it from violating good taste and even common sense. In Jane Austen's *Sense and Sensibility*, the reasonable Edward Ferrars gently mocks Marianne for her self-indulgent, excessive raptures over a bit of "blasted heath" scenery: "I do not like crooked, twisted, blasted trees. I admire them much more if they are tall and flourishing. I do not like ruined, tattered cottages . . . and a troop of tidy, happy villagers please me better than the finest banditti in the world." This is Jane Austen herself speaking in the early nineteenth century for the ordered, controlled patterns of the Age of Reason against the immoderate romantics who had already battered down its walls—its garden walls, as well. Fortunately, each phase left its useful legacy. Brown's carefully planned pseudonaturalism and his landscape plantings, deliberately designed to imitate scenes in paintings, were as artificial as the neoclassicism he destroyed; yet there is no question that England's great landscape parks owe much of their present character to him.

The novels of Sir Walter Scott carried this influence, even intensifying it, into the nineteenth century. But the pendulum was inevitably swinging back, and in 1835 William Cobbett's *The English Garden* showed that balanced formalism was again gaining favor. It was modified by other influences: A brief flirtation with Chinese design can still be seen in the pagoda at Kew; and flowers, which previously had been little used, were now bedded out in what came to be called "mosaic culture," a term descriptive of the tightly planted, neatly contained flower beds massed in carefully balanced designs near houses. These were meant to be viewed from a terrace, if possible, and

against a backdrop of the great park if the house ran to such grandeur. But with the industrial revolution came the homes of the new middle class, which had to content themselves with modest versions of the "bedding-out" style—sometimes reduced to a showy ornamental planting in the middle of a lawn. In order to maintain constant bloom in these masses of color, greenhouses and conservatories burgeoned throughout the country.

By the last years of the nineteenth century, English gardens had more or less sloughed off or absorbed faddish extremes, and settled into a natural kind of development which persists to the present. Formal gardens whose outlines were set down generations ago remain formal in feeling, but are different in detail. They encompass more flowers—frequently in the ubiquitous "herbaceous borders," vividly planted strips framing the justly famous lawns, which have taken the place of the bedding-out style. They accommodate different trees and

Labyrinthine garden at Dieren, in Holland, as it appeared about 1700.

35

Pierre Du Pont established Longwood Gardens (top) at Kennett Square, Pennsylvania, in 1906. Dumbarton Oaks Park (below) adds beauty to Washington, D.C. Opposite: Deane garden at Williamsburg, Virginia.

shrubs, and conform more closely to the basic English view of what a garden should offer: a place in which the owner can get close to, keep a proprietary eye on, and enjoy his piece of land, great or small.

Gardening in America has been the beneficiary of all the accumulated styles of the European and, to some extent, the Oriental past. The earliest settlers, of necessity, could not worry about pleasure gardens when all their energies were bent toward getting the unfamiliar ground to yield food. But each succeeding wave of newcomers brought plants and seeds from the old country, and by the middle of the seventeenth century women had dooryard gardens in

which they set forth plants that had survived the voyage alongside the wealth of wildflowers that they brought in from the fields and hills. Expertly tended by the Dutch, peonies, hollyhocks, eglantine, anemones, lilac, and other imports flourished in these early gardens. The botanist Adrian van der Donck, reporting these successes back to Holland, noted also that some of the native plants the colonists were cultivating were worth attention: sunflowers, new kinds of lilies, lady's-slipper, and a plant he called morning-star which remains uncertainly identified. Other popular indigenous plants were black-eyed Susans, blue and summer phlox, and asters.

36

Excitement over the newly revealed wealth of American plant treasures had already seeped back to Europe. Before the Lewis and Clark expedition of 1804-06 provided botanical along with all its other information about the West, only the wild plants of the eastern regions were available, but even these were enough to revitalize Old World gardens. Travelers like van der Donck and John Josselyn, whose *New England's Rarities Discovered in Birds, Beasts, Fishes, Serpents and Plants in that Country* was published in 1672, were really early ecologists, describing the wildlife they observed as well as the first gardens. Unfortunately, or perhaps intriguingly, we do not always know what they were talking about, for many of the old flower names are not the ones we use today. Most of them we can identify. Hollyhocks, for example, were stock-rosen (meaning pole roses). The carnation was a pink, or a clove, or a gilly-flower; but the gillyflower might also have been a wallflower or a variety of stock. The name itself, gillyflower, may have derived from the Dutch *jenoffelen*, or the French *giroflée*, meaning clove; but it may have come from the old English "July-flower." When van der Donck mentions bellflowers, we cannot be sure what he saw, for to the Dutch a gentian, a columbine, a wild morning-glory could have been a bellflower; the red cardinal, one of America's most striking wildflowers, was a bellflower to the English herbalist Parkinson, and for all we know it could have been so to van der Donck as well.

The early dooryard gardens also grew cooking herbs and vegetables, and were completely informal. But under the Dutch patroon system, which granted tax exemption along such rivers as the Hudson to any

group of more than fifty settlers, the beginnings of a land aristocracy had already appeared in the seventeenth century. And as money accumulated, the owners of more elaborate homes attempted formal gardens patterned on the European and English ones they remembered. In Virginia and Maryland, plantations re-created the English manor-house scene. How important the land was to those country gentlemen is made apparent when we learn that while commanding his troops George Washington took time to send home to Mount Vernon a detailed list of trees he wanted set out "in proper time" the coming fall. Thomas Jefferson was another gentleman farmer-gardener whose mountain-top home, Monticello, was a personal creation. Jefferson's exhaustive garden notebooks have

guided the restoration of Monticello's gardens and have been invaluable also in recreating other seventeenth-and eighteenth-century gardens, like those in the marvelous restoration of Williamsburg.

Landowners like Washington and Jefferson helped, but another group of men were largely responsible for much of the botanical knowledge, and hundreds of new plants that came from the newly opened continent and stimulated a rich transatlantic traffic. Most of these men were, like the Tradescants, English. John Clayton, who had explored Virginia, made a collection of plants which formed the basis for *Flora Virginica* by John F. Gronovius. Mark Catesby spent more than seven years on the eastern shores of America before returning to England to write a *Natural History of Carolina, Florida and the Bahama Islands.* Among his plant discoveries are the American begonia, the catalpa, and the scarlet-flowered acacia.

The name that overshadows the others, however, is Bartram—again like the Tradescants, a father-and-son combination which added up to an entire century of botanical exploration and enrichment. John Bartram (1699-1777) was a plowman, but he became so absorbed in plant study that he left his farm, near Darby, Pennsylvania—and in effect his resentful wife, too—to go to Philadelphia to study botany. By 1731, Bartram had begun America's first botanical garden, remarried, and become the focal point for the Philadelphia naturalists who were the most important and active in the country until the nineteenth century.

With his son William, Bartram followed Indian trails through unmapped country from Lake Erie to Florida, bringing back to his experimental garden specimens so numerous that no definitive list has ever been established. He had a scientist's, not a dilettante's approach; he was the first to apply Linnaeus' system of plant classification, the first to use gypsum as a fertilizer. In the journals he and William kept of their extraordinarily difficult trips, they collected not only botanical information but hundreds of observations on the interrelationships of animals, people, and the land.

It was William who later wrote his father's memoirs, but John will always be remembered for his unique correspondence with the London naturalist-nurseryman, Peter Collinson, a correspondence that included a vast exchange of plants and that enriched both English and American gardens and the literature of friendship, although the two never met.

By the nineteenth century, the clipper-ship trade was introducing many new plants into American gardens. Forsythia, wisteria, fuchsia, dahlia, verbena, and petunia came from South America; geraniums, which seem almost an American trademark, came originally from Africa. But gardens themselves did not develop any style that was particularly American or of the period—possibly because where there was an attempt made at "landscape design" it was usually an imitation of one of the many styles that had occured in other times and places.

A. J. Downing was the first American to assume the title of landscape architect. It is said that Downing was more responsible than any other single individual for the look of a large part of America in his time, but actually he was more an architect and nurseryman than he was a landscape designer, and his effect on the landscape was chiefly through the English Gothic mansions, Swiss chalets, and Italian villas he created rather than through the gardens that accompanied them. Downing seems to have specialized in contradictions; he despised the fake-classical Greek Revival buildings that were popular before he became active, yet in his own home on the Hudson, Highland Gardens, he decorated the formal lawn and terrace with neoclassic urns. He also believed that a house should be an honest dwelling place whose features "expressed their purpose," yet one of his many detractors took pleasure in pointing out that Highland Gardens itself boasted two blind towers that could not conceivably have been put there for any purpose except pretentious decoration. In his grounds, Downing tended toward what is sometimes called the "gardenesque" style—setting out trees and shrubs with an eye to their individual display, without any particular philosophy or design or concern with the total atmosphere. But his taste was greatly esteemed. In 1851 he was hired by the government to design public buildings in Washington, and to plan the grounds for the White House and the new Smithsonian Institution.

One achievement that Downing did not live to see was Central Park in New York City, in which he had an indirect hand. It was actually designed by his young colleague, Calvert Vaux, with Frederick Law Olmsted, and not even begun until 1865. But it incorporated many of Downing's ideas and since he had brought Vaux to this country and had long crusaded for more public parks, it is another reflection of his influence on the American landscape.

For practical purposes American gardens in recent years have developed on three levels. There is the comparatively small group of great private estates. There are gardens that originally were created by and for private owners but have now been given to the public—Longwood in Pennsylvania, for example, and Winterthur in Delaware, both part of the Du Pont Foundation, and Dumbarton Oaks in Washington, D.C. Third, and by far the most important, is the typical suburban garden, which became a national preoccupation—some might say obsession—when the flight to the suburbs began some twenty-odd years ago.

In the early days of suburban living, older houses might be landscaped in a number of ways, but the new developments displayed a kind of style in the openness of their lawns. The lawn rolled down into the lawns of one's neighbors. No hedges, no barriers, no unfriendly fences marred the great green togetherness—which had the accidental advantage of disguising from the passerby exactly how large, or small, one's property really was. This openness having been shown to be impractical, the lines of demarcation now are back, and most landholders have discovered that it is far easier to create attractive grounds within a definite framework.

Fads come and go, of course, but they have only minor and transient effects on the modern American garden. California and the Southwest have, logically, more gardens in the Spanish style than are seen in the East and in the gardens of contemporary houses there is often a Japanese influence. But, in general, American gardens are governed by personal taste, the land's own character and demands, and the limits that time, money, space, and climate must always impose.

3. The Elements

Man is related to plants as all living things are related. Whether animal or vegetable, life is generally believed to have evolved in water from single, simple cells that, through some interaction of chemical and electrical factors, were stimulated into reacting to their environment; into eating, respiring, reproducing; into living. Science has been able to learn considerable about the evolutionary process—with the discovery of the existence of bacteria (which displays both animal- and plant-like characteristics) and from early forms of plant life which still survive, such as the blue-grass algae.

Those first enterprising cells derived energy from the sun, nutrients and oxygen from water and air. They multiplied by fission, and organized in colonies. And eventually, in another mysterious evolutionary thrust to which we do not yet possess the key, some of them found their way onto land. We do not actually know when this occurred; nor will we ever know how many of those early migrants failed, either at the very beginning or as they tried to adapt to the land. Geologists offer fossil remains dating back 420 million years, but they are cautious about identifying these fossils as plant forms.

Sometimes a very early rock layer shows "trace" evidence—tantalizing carbon deposits revealing that some form of life was present. Whether it was plant-like or animal-like, it was too fragile to leave a definite impression and we may never know any more about it.

We know, however, that about forty million years later, lake shores, swamps, and other water-bordering areas were well-covered with the earliest vegetation of which we have reliable evidence: ferns, mosses, and horsetails.

These plants reproduced by spores, tiny cells that collected in closed capsules on their stems, on the undersides of their fronds, and in the tips of the horsetails. When the capsules opened, these spores fell to the ground or were carried by the wind to reproduce elsewhere.

Spores appear to be a wasteful, inefficient means of reproduction, but nonetheless they led to the development of giant ferns and mosses that helped to form the coal beds of the Carboniferous era. And many primitive ferns and grasses still exist, some—like the horsetails and the whisk fern—have survived in a kind of arrested development only slightly changed from the original form. They still have neither true roots nor true leaves, and reproduce by alternating sexual and asexual generations. Their spores, released from protective nodules, grow into plants that contain both male and female sex organs, generally underground where moisture aids fertilization. The resultant plant produces spores and the cycle again repeats itself.

True leaves, which increase a plant's ability to make its own food (one of the more important distinctions between the plant and animal kingdoms) and to take advantage of the atmosphere, did not appear until about 390 million years ago. True seeds appeared with the first conifers, about 345 million years ago. And not until 135 million years ago were there any flowers.

The process has been slow and complex to a degree that is hard to comprehend. Geological evidence makes it fairly certain that more than two billion years were required for those first animate cells to evolve

42

Night and day; moonlight
and sunshine; fog and drops of
morning dew on leaves and flowers;
wind, the turbulence which
carries seeds into new
territory for germination
and growth; once more the sun
going down beyond the
horizon—these are the labors of
nature and the elements
of the turning year which help
to create and maintain
the nourishing green
world of the gardener.

45

into the miracles of scent and color and form with which a gardener can now surround himself. Yet consider an apple tree, each of whose possibly six thousand leaves contains about fifty million cells. There are many more millions of cells in its trunk, roots, and branches. Consider also that from those first cells have developed all the other tremendously complex plant organisms of the contemporary world—an estimated 375 thousand varieties. Viewed in this light, two billion years seems a reasonable amount of time for nature to have taken to produce such results.

Nor, no matter how much we read or how vividly we imagine, can we really visualize those vanished periods. Paleobotanists may tell us about the flowers of the Cretaceous era, but it was not until 100 million years later that men were around to admire them. We are told that this world evolved into our own environment, but we think of it as utterly apart—as remote and alien as a star.

Yet all around us there exists a set of factors that operates now as it did then, providing a comprehensible link between that first cell and our apple tree. No matter how simple, the earliest forms of land vegetable life were as dependent on the elements as the rain forests of Hawaii and the roses in our backyards are today. They all needed water, air, light, and time; they all were affected by temperature and soil.

No flourishing life—either animal or plant—has emancipated itself from its need for the water in which it originated. Water transports hormones, vitamins, minerals, and other essential elements and compounds without which life is impossible. Animals carry a certain amount of water within their bloodstreams, protected by tissue and an elastic,

waterproof skin; when they need to add to this internal supply, they find drinking water —or die. Plants, which need water just as much, find it in different ways. As they cannot travel to it, they must either make their home in it, as water plants do, or take root where enough of it can be drawn from the soil to fill their needs. Though they cannot move, they are adaptable to the extent that if there is water within reach they will fight to get to it; their roots will reach out or down to whatever lengths are necessary. Even desert areas provide moisture for plants that can send roots deep enough to tap underground sources.

Under normal climatic conditions the water within the earth and on its surface is replenished by rain, snow, sleet, and hail. In a never-ending cycle, the sun evaporates surface water, which forms mist and clouds, which in turn burst, sending water back to the earth. If the season is even moderately dry, the gardener's hose must supply what nature has not. Drought, of course, is the great disaster, as catastrophic today as it was when the primitives were propitiating their rain-gods. Even now, when it seems possible that cloud-seeding techniques will enable us to stimulate at least limited rainfall, there are American Indians who use their ancient rain dances as more than mere tourist attractions.

Water does more than feed plants. It plumps out their cells and keeps them rigid;

46

Skunk Cabbage

Wild Sarsaparilla

Lacy pattern of spring trees ↓ Coltsfoot

↓ Celandine ↑ Spring Beauty

Spring:
In this season is the promise
of immortality. The woods' colors are
almost transparent, the flowers
tiny. Violets and spring beauty appear,
ferns show their fronds
and trees the delicate tracery
of their first leaves.

it softens and loosens the soil to provide a better environment for spreading roots; and it helps to convey seeds to new locations. The Aztecs, offering fresh human hearts to their rain-god Tlaloc, paid him homage; they recognized that without the rain maker on their side, it would be impossible for life to go on at all.

The air that surrounds the earth and forms our atmosphere comprises oxygen, nitrogen, carbon dioxide, and other elements in small amounts. It allows men, animals, and plants to breathe—to effect the exchange of gases necessary to their survival. For plants, as well as for animals, air is a basic support of life, but they have nothing similar to an animal's respiratory system with which to make use of it. Its access to plants is through the cellular structure of the leaves.

The discovery that plants "breathed" came in the eighteenth century, when Joseph Priestley and Karl Wilhelm Scheele independently discovered the substance that Antoine Lavoisier later named oxygen. Priestley found that a mouse, confined in a glass container, eventually would die from breathing his own exhaled air. When a green plant was put in with him, however, he remained alive. Obviously the plant did something to the air that kept it fit for animal—and therefore human—consumption. Further experiments

established the process and named the components. In breathing, animals take oxygen from the air and replace it with carbon dioxide, which to them is poisonous. Plants reverse the process, using carbon dioxide and releasing oxygen back into the air.

It appeared from these experiments that plants made the air more healthful for humans, and hospital rooms began to burgeon with bouquets brought to the ailing by well-meaning friends. We continue the custom of taking flowers to sickrooms, but we know now that their function is purely psychological. The leaves are the parts of a plant that breathe air and transpire water, a process influenced by light, temperature, and air movement. This is related to the plant world's most important activity: photosynthesis (meaning "to put together with light") in which the complex green substance called chlorophyll utilizes the sun's energy to manufacture carbohydrates from water and carbon dioxide, releasing oxygen as a by-product. The carbohydrates, as starches or sugars, enter man's diet when he eats fruits and vegetables, and indirectly, but nonetheless crucially, when he eats the flesh of animals that have fed on plant material. It is as essential to the maintenance of human life as are proteins, fats, and minerals. In this sense it is possible to say that all life ultimately rests on the photosynthesizing ability of plants.

Light is crucial to plants in other ways. It stimulates them to their most visible movement: the phototropic movement through which leaves, and sometimes an entire plant, tend to turn toward a source of light. All plants require light, but not all require the same amount. Ferns, many wildflowers, and herbs prefer well-shaded sites. It is useful

Jewelweed

Skullcap

Harebel

Evening Primrose

Yellow Rocket

Swamp-Candle

Summer:

*This is the time
of fulfillment. Growth
is rampant and almost
visible, hopes are
redeemed, and colors
vibrate everywhere.
Now cheeses nestle around
vegetable gardens.*

Spotted Wintergreen

Autumn colors a quiet pond.

Winged Spindle Tree

Autumnal Maple leaf

Rattlesnake Plantain

Woodbine, or Virginia Creeper

Autumn:

It is a burst of glory.
The earth is proud of its
labors, but begins
to tire. Leaves turn,
the cardinal flower blooms,
goldenrod fills the
meadow. Grass is fading
and ferns turn pale.

51

Giuseppe Arcimboldo, 16th-century Milanese artist,
combined a taste for the fantastic with realistic representations
of nature. Left: "Summer. Right: "Water."

for the gardener to know that dogwood, weigela, and some azaleas do better in partial shade than in full sun, while roses, pinks, and carnations want as much bright sunlight as they can get. There are some plants so sensitive to light that they stay closed against it, and open only in the dim light of the moon. The blossoms of angel's trumpet (*Datura*), known to the earliest herbalists as a narcotic, open at dusk and close at sunrise. The buds of the evening primrose open at the end of the day and fade with the morning. The night-blooming cereus, a cactus, puts on a more spectacular performance. It opens only one night every year, stirring at dusk and coming to full bloom around midnight.

The length of time during which light falls on plants, the photoperiod, affects different plants differently. Sunflowers, hibis-cuses, and lettuce bloom only when more than half the day is bright; they are long-day plants. Chrysanthemums and asters respond best to shorter days with longer periods of darkness; they are short-day plants. In a temperate climate, autumn and spring encourage the short-day plants; long-day plants are those of midsummer. Day-neutral plants such as marigolds are relatively unaffected by the photoperiod.

In the eighteenth century, the naturalist Linnaeus (born Carl von Linné) made some interesting observations about the relationship between flowers and light. Linnaeus, whose notable achievement was the binomial identification of flowers by both genus and species which systematized botanical knowledge, found in the course of his studies that certain flowers move, open, and close at certain times of the day. With these data he

52

devised his Floral Clock. According to Linnaeus, this was, in part, the timetable:

Greater Bindweed	3 A.M.
Goatsbeard (Tragopogon)	4 A.M.
Chicory	5 A.M.
White Water Lily	7 A.M.
Marigold	9 A.M.
Star-of-Bethlehem	11 A.M.
Night-flowering Campion	5 P.M.
Morning-Glory	10 P.M.

The idea had charm, but was far from reliable. Any gardener knows that plants can react in highly individual ways to slight differences in environment. Linnaeus did not allow for changes due to fluctuating rainfall or temperature. The over-all observation, however, is correct: Certain flowers do seem to have internal mechanisms that react to certain qualities in the light that reaches them.

Thus water, air, and light are the elemental forces that sustain earth's vegetation. Their interrelationship with the plant world is basic, as important to a garden today as it was to the pine-like trees on which the Triassic dinosaurs may have nibbled.

Three other factors influence plant life: temperature, time, and soil. Temperature is vitally important to plants, which cannot change their situations as animals can. A man in a cold draft can move to a warmer place; a plant either adapts to the draft or dies. In this sense, temperature is almost a function of time, for it is the length of time over which a favorable accumulation of temperature occurs that allows a plant to mature.

Time and temperature have both external and internal influences on vegetation. The warming light that falls on a plant heats the air around it as well as the soil in which it grows, further affecting its well-being. In zonal areas that are fairly clear and consistent around the world, certain plants will be found because certain temperature-time conditions are found. Tropical plants are those that thrive in warmth the year round. Temperate-zone plants, bounded by the first and last killing frosts, appear to need not only shorter periods of warmth but also the change of seasons. Many fruit trees and spring-flowering bulbs survive only in climates that provide cool autumns and cold winters in which they can lie dormant before the increasing warmth of spring encourages them to stir again. Above the timberline on mountains, where it is too cold for trees to grow, alpine flowers, mosses, and lichens manage to survive. There are even some stubborn, hardy lichens that find purchase on rocks on the snow-covered mountaintop—the arctic zone that provides the most nearly impossible growing environment of all.

The enveloping biosphere—land, water, air, temperature—that controls the earth's natural vegetation controls the gardener as well. He can modify his garden environment to some extent: provide shelter for a wind-sensitive begonia, or create a sun-trapping area for a special rose. Unless there is a regional drought, he can always supplement inadequate rainfall. But, basically, he must accept the limitations of climate and seasonal change.

In the total ecology of plants there is one factor that the gardener can influence. He can do something about the soil. Its consistency, depth, and nutritive content are vitally important to his plants, and—to a greater degree than he can modify any other factor—the gardener can modify the soil.

According to its chemical makeup, soil

Winter:

Snowstorm buries a dormant
garden and softens
stark outline of dogwood branch.
Right: Heavy coating of
ice often fractures
tree limbs, but is one of
the lovely sights
of winter when sun is shining
in a cloudless sky.

redded bark

Leaves

Wood chips

Peanut shells   ↓ Soil

↑ "Dirt"   ↓ Cocoa beans   ↓ Compost piles

Soils & Mulches:

Without soil-enriching mulches and additives, no garden can make much of a showing. Laboratory experiments and age-old experience have combined to discover appropriate mixtures for our diverse plants.

is classified as acid, alkaline, or neutral. According to its structure, it is described as sand, silt, or clay, each of which has different water-holding and food-preserving qualities. The best garden soil is a mixture of sand, clay, and humus, resulting in a loam porous enough to allow for drainage and fertile enough to nourish plants to top performance. This kind of soil can conceivably be made overnight with chemicals, additives, and synthetic substances that come fairly close to turning poor soil into an approximation of the real thing. This is fortunate, for the "real thing" is being destroyed and eroded, generation by generation. It is the soil that has laid in forests, at the base of mountains, in open meadows, and in wildernesses for millions of years, enriched by weather, animals, and the substance of decayed plant matter. This good black earth is topsoil, and without it or a reasonable facsimile the gardener is hopelessly handicapped. But the facsimile, if he is willing to work, is within his grasp.

Humus, the vegetable mold resulting from decomposing organic matter, is the key ingredient. It increases the soil's water-holding ability and helps it to absorb the sun's energy. It releases mineral compounds which nurture the plants. It retains and makes available to the plants any soluble plant foods the gardener adds in the form of commercial fertilizer. The gardener can add humus to his soil most readily by mixing it with partially decomposed plant material known as peat. It can be obtained in several ways: one hard and two comparatively easy. The dedicated gardener can take his shovel into the nearest forest bog and dig his own supply; afterwards he may be willing to settle for one of the easier ways. The

A black and naked tree, solitary in the gray winter landscape, stands against a snow-laden sky and gives silent promise of brighter days to come.

first merely involves a trip to a good nursery, where compressed peat, easy to transport and easy to mix with his own soil, will be available. The second way involves more time and work: Peat can be made in a compost heap, made by the gardener by piling leaves, allowing them to mold, and adding other natural materials to further enrich the nutritive content. It is even possible to start with a base of what roadworkers forthrightly call "dirt," and to add peat, additional leaf mold, grass cuttings, and even vegetable and animal garbage (if the compost heap is far enough from the house) to create a very creditable soil additive. If the mixture is allowed to mold long enough, it even can be used as soil itself. In effect, the private gardener is following the lead of commercial growers, who add tanbark, coconut shell, wood chips, and other materials to create from mediocre soil the vast quantities of richly nutritive, workable soil they need.

In the deep-seated, tenacious love for the earth that no amount of cement and stone seems able to block from man's consciousness, there is surely the atavistic knowledge that once he gets his hands into the dirt, man is somehow in league with life. For the true gardener the reward lies precisely there—he can change the soil, improve it, cause things to grow from it that would not have come up without his help. It is one of the very few ways in which he can come close to allying himself with the creative forces that control his existence.

4. Cycle d

A successful garden in spring and summer bloom is a collection of delights. We are dazzled by color, excited by scent, astonished by the variety of form, texture, and design. It is hard for the gardener to acknowledge that all this beauty exists not to gratify his senses but to ensure its own propagation. Yet it is biologically true. Flowers exist to produce seeds and, through pollination of the seeds, new plants. Struggling like all living things to remain alive and to beget new life, flowers please man only incidentally and by accident.

Nature's earliest efforts to propagate vegetation by means of spores were somewhat hit-or-miss. But from the spore-reproducing ferns and horsetails that are still with us, we can see why they were not unsuccessful. The dust-like spores were produced and released in such quantities that, although they were totally at the mercy of wind and chance, at least some of them were bound to come down on adequate growing sites. Their minute size is an advantage: Spores find anchorage in hairline cracks and in crannies between rocks that would never nourish a seed. And so, they survived.

With some later plants, where sex differentiation had occurred, fertilization took place when rainwater conveyed a male cell to a female cell. These cells, however, were naked. The plants they grew into produced nothing resembling our blossoms. Then, 135 million years ago, flowers began to appear—mallow, magnolia, and buttercup among the earliest. One of nature's most mysterious achievements, the covered seed, had evolved.

From an evolutionary point of view, it is interesting that, efficient as seeds are, nature utilizes a variety of other reproductive processes. Not all contemporary plants reproduce by seed, or by seed alone. Some are propagated by vegetative reproduction, either occurring in nature or through man's agency as he grafts buds and roots cuttings taken from plants that lend themselves to this kind of growth. Suckers, corms, and stolons are other plant parts from which new plants can be made. Many garden plants—tulip, hyacinth, narcissus, and others—are grown from bulbs, which are underground storage compartments containing food and modifications of stems and leaves. Iris and the orange day lily are among the plants grown from rhizomes, the thickened, rootlike, partially uncovered stems that produce roots and leaves and can be divided by the most inexperienced gardener to help create new growth.

Nevertheless, by far the major portion of present-day flora is produced by the covered seed. It is the beginning and end of a yearly cycle: It goes into the ground, and germinates into a plant whose end product is a new growth of seeds.

Seeds have developed in infinite variety, in a constant interaction with soil, climate, and growing conditions which has, over generations, tailored their sizes, shapes, and viability to best serve the needs of the plants they must reproduce. Their size range is astonishing. Some are minute, like the pinpoint seeds of alyssum and petunia. But the double coconut, which may weigh up to sixty pounds, is also a seed—the largest known. A seed's covering can be thin, as it is on the green bean, and fragile as the papery brown covering of the peanut. Or it can range from the tough coating of the orange pip to the stony armor that protects the Brazil nut. Seeds can be dispersed by a dozen

60

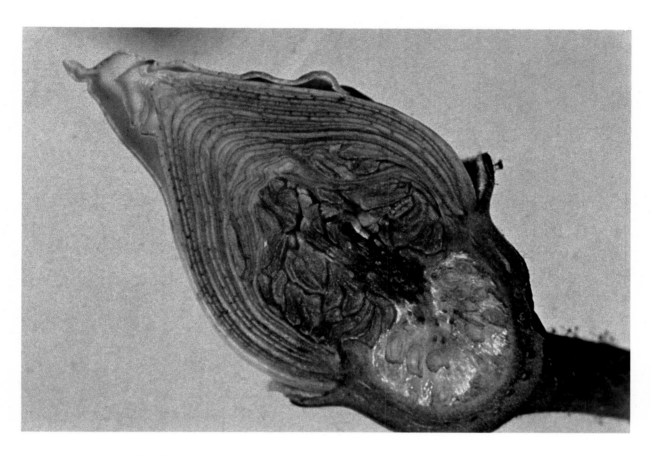

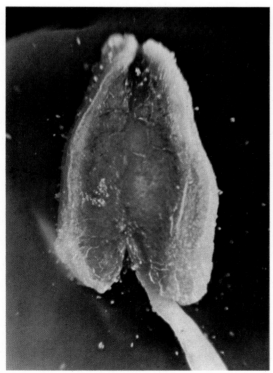

Opening pages:
Horizontal cut through
rosebud reveals
neat arrangement of
future petals.
Above: Vertical cut
through rosebud.
Far left: Microscopic
view of anther
from rose stamen.
Left: Sepals of opening
bud will soon be
smaller than full flower.

different ways, by many agents: by wind and water, by birds and insects, by animals, and by man.

Any small, light seed is easily conveyed by wind. To adapt even better to this kind of dispersal, some seeds have developed wings, like those of the ash tree, or plumes and tufts, like the milkweed, dandelion, and thistle. Many kinds of seeds, and even whole fruits, are ferried by rain, or carried for long distances by streams or rivers. If a seed is protected by a relatively solid coating it may even be relocated by a flood or by the ocean itself. Coconuts are believed to have been carried by ocean currents to a wide range of new and amenable sites.

Seeds are carried by animals in several ways: Small ones may adhere to the mud on their hoofs or pads, others may catch onto animals' fur. Both birds and animals spread seeds when, having eaten the fruit or plant that contains them, they wander along and drop their waste elsewhere.

Man's seed-spreading contribution has been vital. From the semibarbaric conquerors of remote times to the contemporary plant explorers who wander through hidden areas of the Andes to find new specimens, man has always brought growing things back from his travels as though they were treasure. In the great migrations and in later pilgrimages, displaced peoples took with them, when they could, seed or plants that would serve to link the new home with the old. Often, too, as with animals, the seeds came with man by accident: on the soles of his boots, the wheels of his conveyances, even the tools he carried.

If there is a beginning in this endless chain, it is perhaps in the soil where the seed is buried. There it germinates, sending roots outward and downward to grope for the necessary nourishment. As the plant breaks through the soil, the roots serve also as its anchor. A well-nourished plant sends up a firm stem, which may branch into several parts. From the stem grow the leaves, on whose food-making photosynthetic activity the expanding life of the plant—and indirectly the life of man—depends. Through transpiration, a process by which some of the moisture drawn up by the roots is released into the air, leaves help to cool and moisten the atmosphere. The leaf of a plant is as distinctive as its flower; any plant can be identified by its leaves alone. But leaves also are amazingly distinctive from each other; like human fingerprints, no two leaves are exactly alike.

Root, stem, leaf—all play their essential parts in keeping the plant alive and strong. But the flower unquestionably has the starring role. It is the custodian of potential new life, its generating agent through fertilization, and its protector until it is ready to go into the earth to renew the cycle.

A flower is made of leaflike sepals, which form a cup called the calyx. Inside the calyx are the petals, collectively known as the corolla. The flower's male organs, the stamens, grow out of the calyx. They are slender stalks in whose enlarged tips, the anthers, the pollen grains are secreted. From the center of the flower grows the female organ, the pistil, a somewhat thicker, more rigid stalk on whose tip, or stigma, the pollen will be deposited. The stigma may be rough, smooth, sticky, or feathery, according to the kind of pollen it is designed to receive. The base of the pistil enlarges into the ovary, in which the immature seeds, the ovules, await fertilization. Nothing can hap-

Top left: Lady's-slipper cut away to show trapped bee pollinating flower. Top right: Pollinia of Everglades orchid is stuck to tip of match. Below: Bees frolicking in coreopsis.

63

Left: 1. Dragonfly hovering over plantain. 2. Butterfly taking nectar from milkweed blossoms. 3. Beetle in Indian blanket. 4. Close-up of veins of dogwood leaf. 5. Pinna of interrupted fern. 6. Pistils and stamen form tulip's sexual apparatus.

Right: Abraham Mignon, little-known 17th-century German painter, depicts in lifelike forms the living elements of the gardener's world. Title: "Flowers, Animals and Insects."

Right: Seedpod of a poppy, a beautifully symmetrical design. Opposite: Alder catkin shedding pollen which will be carried by wind to new locations.

pen until acceptable pollen grains make contact with a receptive stigma. When this occurs, the pollen grain germinates on the stigma and sends a tube, through which it discharges sperm cells, down into the ovary. The time between germination and fertilization can vary from as little as one hour in barley to a matter of months in such shrubs as witch hazel. As the fertilized seeds develop, the ovary enlarges; the petals fall; and the plant is only one step removed from total fulfillment—the use of its seeds to produce new plants.

From a reproductive standpoint, the "perfect" flower is a hermaphrodite that carries both male and female parts. Some of our most common flowers are complete in this sense: daisies, sunflowers, buttercups, tulips, roses, gentians. Imperfect, or unisexual, flowers (the holly's, for example) may be either staminate, male, or pistillate, female. Some plants typically bear both kinds of unisexual flowers at the same time: oaks, beeches, pumpkins, cucumbers, many begonias. Nature has also found room for sterile flowers, which bear no functioning sex organs. These often spectacular flowers may occur, as they do in the cornflower, on a plant that also carries hermaphrodite or unisexual blossoms and are apparently de-signed to help attract pollinators.

Pollination can occur within a hermaphroditic flower, or between different flowers on the same plant. This self-pollination is not considered desirable by some botanists, since it is a form of inbreeding and, as with animals, better varieties and stronger new organisms tend to result when male and female are not related. Yet it occurs with many vegetables and has resulted in some of our most beautiful orchids. Self-sterility, in which a plant cannot be fertilized by its own pollen, may be one of nature's attempts at restricting self-pollination. An estimated three thousand plants, some of them as important to man as the apple tree, will respond only to pollen from another plant. As a result, man has become one of nature's most active cross-pollinators, improving by his skill not only the beauty of his gardens but the yield and quality of his food resources.

Wind is responsible for some pollination, man for much more; but the chief agent remains, as always, insects (and, to a lesser degree, birds). A flower's scent and color are designed to attract these essential visitors.

The process is far from one-sided. As the bee collects or deposits pollen, the flower is feeding him. The associations are so intimate and specialized that certain insects go chiefly, and consistently, to certain flowers; each is equipped by nature to best serve the needs of the other. Water lilies are pollinated by beetles; their large flowers can withstand the beetle's weight and roughness. Butterflies travel among lighter, more fragile blossoms. Whenever there is a trumpet vine there will be a hummingbird whose long, thin beak is a perfect instrument for probing the long throat of the trumpet flower. As can be seen from the list that follows, flowers and insects exist in a state of cooperation that benefits both; it is possible that without this neither would exist in the forms we now know.

Pollination

WIND-pollinated flowers

POLLEN grains are lightweight, rounded, and smooth.

FLOWERS are small, inconspicuous in color, lack odor and nectar.

Examples: Ragweed, Pigweeds, Cattail, Grasses, Box elder, Oaks, Conifers, Alders, Walnuts, Hickories, Poplars, Birches.

INSECT-pollinated flowers

POLLEN grains are rough, irregular, sticky, and heavy.

FLOWERS are white or brightly colored; odor and/or nectar is present.

BUTTERFLIES: Pinks, Silenes, Buddleia, Purple loosestrife, Violets, Heaths, Laurel, Phlox, Mints, Monarda, Toadflax, Joe-pye weed, Yarrow, Thistle, Umbelliferae, Dogbane.

BEETLES: Magnolia, Calycanthus, Peonies, American chestnut, Elderberry, Queen Anne's lace, Cow parsnip, Water lilies.

HONEYBEES (blind to red but not ultra-violet): Skunk cabbage, Virginia creeper, Iris, Crucifers, Bindweed, Dogbane, Horse chestnut, Pussy willow, Violets, Canada lily, Poppies, Milkweed, English ivy, Linden, Heaths, Mints, Asters, Legumes, Wild geranium, Wild roses, cultivated fruit trees and shrubs of Rose family, Barberry, May apple, Lady's-slipper.

WASPS: Goldenrods, Milkweeds.

BUMBLEBEE: Lady's-slipper, Red clover, Solomon's-seal, Trout lily, Iris, Horse chestnut, Scotch broom, Trailing arbutus, Corydalis, Wild columbine, Monkshood, Bar-

berry, Dutchman's-breeches, Bloodroot, Jewelweed, Bindweed, Phlox, Mints, Butter-and-eggs, Thistle, Wood betony, Asters.

HAWK MOTHS: Honeysuckle, Butter-and-eggs, Orchis, Rhododendron, Phlox, Soapwort, Silenes, Orchids, Tobacco, Evening Primrose, Turk's-cap-lily, Bindweed, Petunia.

BEEFLY (BOMBYLIUS): Dandelion, Grape hyacinth, Clematis, Bloodroot, Milkweed, Asters, Monkey flower.

CARRION FLIES: Skunk cabbage, Jack-in-the-pulpit, Pitcher plant, Wake-robin.

GNATS: Dutchman's-pipe by Chironomidae; Jack-in-the-pulpit by Mycetophia.

SYRPHID FLIES: Umbellifers, Veronica, Irises, Marsh marigold, Crucifers, Saxifrages, Legumes, Wild geranium, Mints.

SPECIAL ASSOCIATIONS: Yucca requires the Yucca moth; Figs require a gall wasp.

HUMMINGBIRD: Cardinal flower, Hibiscus, Trumpet vine, Honeysuckle, Petunia, cultivated Impatiens, Mexican century plant.

BAT: Tropicals only—Sausage tree (*Kigelia*), Calabash, Balsa, Kapok, Durian, some species of Banana.

(This list was compiled by Eleanor Ivanye Fanning, author of *Insects Close-Up*.)

5. From the Wildernes

Woods and Waters

A wildflower garden is a contradiction in terms. A garden is man-made, while wildflowers are strictly speaking those that originate and grow without human intervention. They are not set into special places. They are not cared for by gardeners or botanists. They are not propagated, pruned, hybridized, fertilized, or cultivated by human skill or whim. They are planted by wind, insects, and all the other agents of propagation. They are nourished by the earth and controlled by the elements and the seasons. They find their own best environments, colonize with other plants with which they can coexist, and even adapt when necessary to altered circumstances—many of them caused by man's invasion. And through the genius and force of nature alone, they survive wherever civilization has not set too heavy a foot.

They will even survive civilization, as long as man leaves a patch of earth behind. Almost everywhere in the world, great highway networks smother soil; the courses of mighty rivers are altered; and, to make room for new houses, trees are felled, meadows violated, and the good black earth made into dust. But as soon as the bulldozers leave, the flowers are back on any bit of ground offering purchase for their roots—quite a miracle, considering the amount of damage man does and how much he shortsightedly destroys as he "builds."

The persistence of these plants of the wilderness is heartening, for it offers hope that generations to come still will be able to marvel at the beauty of a cardinal flower and compare the fragile wild rose with its sophisticated descendants. But as man pushes relentlessly outward, the marginal wilderness diminishes and we lose contact with nature, with peace, with innocence. We need somehow to keep the free, wild mountains and woods and waters close to our metal-and-glass everyday lives.

Wildflower preserves do part of the job. All over the country, farsighted towns are beginning to maintain parks with nature walks where children can learn that geraniums do not always come complete with pots, as on apartment window sills, and where they understand the difference between a Christmas and a maidenhair fern, and why a starflower and a star-of-Bethlehem, though similar, are entirely different plants.

But is it not up to the gardener—the person who says he loves flowers—to help take a hand in preserving this wild beauty, some of it already close to extinction? He can do part of the job; he can create his own wildflower preserve. He can go into the woods and fields and bring wildflowers back to his own piece of ground. It need only be a wooded corner, a rocky ledge, a pond—as long as it re-creates the environment.

Some of the problems and techniques of making a wildflower garden are discussed in Chapter Eight. Here we suggest a few flowers, shrubs, and trees that have the best chance of succeeding in a man-made garden.

Inevitably, there will be disappointments, but counterbalancing them is a list of pleasures that cannot be derived from "store-bought" plants: the woodland exploration, the thrill of identification, the discovery, one spring morning, that the trailing arbutus that seemed on the point of giving up is going to make it after all. And above all this is the gardener's satisfying conviction that he is working against destruction, helping nature in its struggle to survive.

Preceding pages: Still-existing American wilderness. Opposite: Detail of Botticelli's "Primavera" contains flowers which may be found in many lands today.

70

Pinxter

Columbine

↑ Wild Iris ↓ Madonna Lily

↑ Euphorbia ↓ Woodland Violet

Of course, generations of crossbreeding and hybridizing of the plants man has taken from the wilderness have done no harm. On the contrary, they have given us hundreds of new plants, many new colors, and different shapes than existed before. Azaleas and lilies, for example, and irises and columbines, are among the plants that demonstrate how man has worked with nature. They bloom in our gardens now in splendid size, strength, and variety which, in spite of nature's own facility at propagation, would in all likelihood never have taken form without man's knowledge, skill, and love. They are brilliant reminders that in his encounters with nature, man need not always be the destroyer.

Azaleas, one of the more than seven hundred and fifty species of the Rhododendron family, are native to southern Europe, eastern Asia, and North America, and have been cultivated so skillfully that dozens of spectacular varieties can be bought at any nursery. One of the first wild plants that was successful in the United States was *Rhododendron nudiflorum*, which the Dutch in Pennsylvania named the Pinxter, or Whitsun Flower. Wild Pinxter, a breathtaking sight in full bloom, can still be found in woods and swampy places, and is transplantable if a very small plant is selected and if the greatest care is taken to reproduce the original habitat.

Lilies may be the oldest domesticated flower; certainly their history goes back as far as that of any plant we know. The current name *Lilium* comes from the Celtic *li*, meaning whiteness. But the word *Shûsan*, or *Shôssanah*, means lily in Hebrew, and five thousand years ago in Akkad, where a language similar to Hebrew was spoken,

there was a city called Susa. Thus it appears that the Akkadians grew lilies, or a lily-like flower—further support for the historical speculation that the great Cretan civilization in the Mediterranean was created by wanderers from the Near East, for the lily was sacred to the ancient Cretan goddess Britomartis, and appears in a form we can identify on Cretan pottery and wall paintings. From those early times the lily symbolized motherhood, fruitfulness, and light, and so came naturally to its medieval Christian association with the Virgin Mary.

Lilies are still encountered wild in open woods, but it is now a great adventure to find them, for many native varieties are headed toward extinction. The Wood or Philadelphia Lily (*L. philadelphicum*) is an American original that persisted for a time along country roads that wound through woods, but is now increasingly rare. It is typical of many woodland plants that once grew in the depths of the wilderness, only to become roadside plants as the great cities expanded and thrust their suburbs through the countryside. When there still is woodland soil along the roadsides, these plants can adapt to their newly exposed sites, but they cannot survive being wrenched up by picnickers and children. Even in wildflower preserves where the understanding is clearly *"Do not pick, do not destroy,"* the caretakers tell of plants pulled up by the roots and then, as often as not, carelessly scattered as the vandals found them too much trouble to carry home. And sometimes these are rare specimens that have been established only after seasons of back-breaking effort.

But the Wood Lily and several others of the more than two thousand lily species have survived in North America. The yellow

↑ *Baneberry*　　↓ *Black Snakeroot*

↓ *Dutchman's-Breeches*　　↑ *Bloodroot*　　↓ *White Trillium*

↓ *Solomon's-Seal*

the most part, be obtained in any cultivated form, or in any way other than by the gardener's own time, effort, trained eye, and trowel. They have been selected because they will almost always repay his efforts by surviving; they are grouped, for convenience, by color. While some will grow in relatively exposed places, most are plants that must be sought in sheltered and hidden spots of the woods and waters.

WHITE TO CREAM

BANEBERRY (*Actaea pachypoda*, Buttercup family), also called Cohosh, is a bushy plant found in the deep woods. After the flowering season from April to June, the Baneberry develops clusters of hard, round white berries, each with a purple dot, which so much resemble the china eyes of old-fashioned dolls that for generations the plant has been called "Doll's-eyes." Children, who love it for this reason, should be warned that the berries are poisonous.

BLOODROOT, or INDIAN PAINT (*Sanguinaria canadensis*, Poppy family) is a single-blossom plant that blooms in early spring. Its rhizome contains an orange-red juice that stains whatever it touches and was used by the Indians for dye and war paint. In some parts of the country, sugar lumps dipped into this juice used to be administered as an old-time cough remedy.

CANADA MAYFLOWER (*Maianthemum canadense*, Buttercup family), also called False or Wild Lily of the Valley, is an American native, found in the springtime from Labrador south to North Carolina. It spreads a low-growing carpet of white and green in dense woods and over rocks, and can be trained to blanket mossy boulders in a rock garden.

DUTCHMAN'S-BREECHES (*Dicentra cucullaria*, Fumitory family) resemble tiny pantaloons when viewed with a vivid imagination. Usually found in deep woods, sometimes in clearings, they are a charming addition to a garden because butterflies (as well as insects with long proboscises) cannot resist the nectar-laden flowers.

GOLDTHREAD (*Coptis groenlandica*, Crowfoot family) grows in dark, moist woods in the northern United States and Canada. It flowers in spring. The name derives from the creeping gold-colored root, which is used medicinally and as a bitter flavoring. Steeped in boiling water, it makes a digestive tonic or mouthwash.

MAY APPLE (*Podophyllum peltatum*, Barberry family) was among the easiest North American woodland plants to be domesticated. It will grow almost anywhere, and spreads easily, so that its umbrella-like leaves and its beautiful cream-white flowers soon cover the ground. In July, it produces an oval yellowish fruit—edible, but with an unpleasant, sweetish taste. The fruit has purgative qualities—it was used in this way by the Indians—but in large quantities can prove fatal. The rootstock is definitely poisonous. The May Apple is closely related to the dreaded Mandrake, whose history of evil goes back to Genesis. Theophrastus, Dioscorides, and Pliny all told of its sinister magical qualities, and the superstition that its forked root was the body of an accursed human being persisted until quite recent times.

SOLOMON'S-SEAL (*Polygonatum canaliculatum*, Lily family) is a graceful plant that transplants well to shady banks. Under its soft hairy leaves hang small greenish-white bells, which turn into dark blue ber-

Sessile-leaved Bellwort

Clintonia

Wood Betony

Yellow Lady's-Slippers

Trailing Arbutus

Pink Lady's-Slipper

↑ *Wild Bleeding Heart* ↓ *Blue Lobelia*

Bee Balm

↑ *Red Trillium* ↓ *Hepatica*

Bergamot ↓ Wild Phlox Wild Geranium Jack-in-the-Pulpit

ries in the fall. After fruiting, the stem withers and drops away from the parent rootstock, leaving a round scar that suggests the design of a royal seal, thus its name.

TRILLIUM (*Trillium grandiflorum;* Lily family) is an aristocrat of the woodlands, considered one of America's most attractive wildflowers. The large flowers are so brilliantly white that they can be seen from a distance, and age into an even lovelier pink. Vigorous and easily established in proper environments, the Trillium is one of the American natives now flourishing in English gardens. The *grandiflorum* is the most impressive of the Trilliums, but a number of other varieties grow in North America and a Trillium collection could become an ambitious gardener's hobby. The *Trillium erectum,* to take only one example, is among the few brownish flowers nature has provided us, interesting for the gardener who wants a contrast for the more ordinary garden colors.

TURTLEHEAD (*Chelone glabra;* Snapdragon family) is a native of American swamps and stream banks from Newfoundland to Georgia, and easily identified because its hooded flowers actually do look like turtle or snake heads. In spite of this, the white Turtlehead and its cousins—purpletipped, violet-purple, pink—are attractive additions to the garden. In days gone by, its lance-shaped, saw-edged leaves were used to treat liver ailments.

VIOLET (*Viola blanda;* Violet family) belongs to a family that seems far larger than it is (about eight hundred species) because some member of it grows in every part of the world, even in the Arctic and Antarctic. There are probably as many legends about the Violet as there are species.

To the Greek goddess Persephone, who was picking violets when Pluto snatched her away into the underworld, it seemed accursed. When the weary Orpheus sat down to rest, violets sprang up on the mossy bank beside his lute. The Athenians loved it so much they took the Violet as their symbol and, according to Theophrastus, became so skillful at cultivating it that they could supply the markets all year round. The Greeks used violets for garlands, decorations, and perfume, but, in other times and places, they have been eaten as well. In the Middle Ages they were cooked into puddings. Even now, candied violets are a specialty with some confectioners, and Syrians and Turks use them in sherbet. The perfume is perennially popular. In France, where violets have been favored since the sixth century when Queen Radegond first grew them in the nunnery at Poitiers, hundreds of tons of the flowers go into a single year's perfume production.

Of the fifty or so American species, *V. blanda,* the Sweet White Violet, is especially popular because of its delicate fragrance. But the light blue *V. palmata* is also easily found and well worth transplanting.

WOOD ANEMONE or WINDFLOWER (*Anemone quinquefolia;* Buttercup family) is an American native that grows modest and small in the woods, but will spread its white flowers handsomely in a garden.

YELLOW TO ORANGE

SESSILE-LEAVED BELLWORT (*Uvularia sessilifolia;* Lily-of-the-Valley family) is a lovely American plant that is often overlooked. Its yellowish-green bells blend with the dead leaves among which it grows and

Mandrake, endowed throughout history with mystical powers, is seen in traditional man-like form in copy of Dioscorides medical treatise of first century A.D.

the pale greens of April, but in a woodlike garden area it will spread and surprise the gardener season after season with delicate shape and color.

CLINTONIA (*Clintonia borealis*; Lily family) may be easily recognized by its large, glossy oval leaves. Asa Gray, in naming it for Governor De Witt Clinton of New York, outraged Henry Thoreau, who said that if a small woodland plant had to be named for a man, it should at least be for a man of flowers, not a politician. But Thoreau was missing the point, for De Witt Clinton was an avid naturalist who stole all the time he could to spend in the woods and fields. The Clintonia grows in cool woods, sometimes quite high in the mountains, and will transplant well if not taken too far from its natural surroundings.

INDIAN CUCUMBER ROOT (*Medeola virginiana*; Lily family) in late spring bears an inconspicuous greenish-yellow flower under umbrella-like leaves and in the fall vivid purple berries. The shape and flavor of the edible, tuberous rootstock are responsible for the English name, but the derivation of the Latin is obscure. It was evidently named for the sorceress Medea, who reputedly was skillful with both medicines and poisons; but the Indian Cucumber Root seems to be innocuous in both respects. Its chief distinction—besides the fact that it transplants well—is that it is the only known member of its genus.

WOOD BETONY (*Pedicularis canadensis*; Snapdragon family) is also called Lousewort, because a louse-borne skin disease formerly was reported to afflict sheep after they had browsed on its fernlike foliage, but this unpleasant accusation has never been proved. European Betony, in fact, has a cen-

turies-old reputation for all kinds of good works. Worn about the neck, it was supposed to ward off evil; made into salves, oils, and syrups, it was recommended for almost any illness known to man. Whether or not Wood Betony has other virtues, its unusual color—the blossoms range from true yellow to dark red, even to brown—make it a most interesting transplant to the wildflower garden.

YELLOW LADY'S-SLIPPER (*Cypripedium calceolus*; Orchid family), better known in some areas as the Moccasin

Pink Water Lily

↑ White Water Lily ↓ Pond Lily

↑ Marsh Marigold   ↓ Pickerelweed

Flower, belongs to an enormous family whose seventeen thousand species are scattered over the world from the Arctic to the tropics. This one is found from Newfoundland south to the mountains of Georgia. Lady's-slippers of varied color are native to both Europe and the North American woods, but the sparkling, purple-lined yellow of this variety makes it outstanding.

PINK TO RED

BEE BALM or OSWEGO TEA (*Monarda didyma*, Mint family) is one of the few scarlet plants of the North American woods. Bumblebees love it, for their long "tongues" are capable of scooping up the nectar stored at the base of the deep-throated flower; the needle-billed hummingbirds also flock wherever Bee balm grows. Early settlers learned from the Indians to make a soothing tea from the Bee balm's aromatic leaves and flowers.

BERGAMOT or HORSEMINT (*Monarda fistulosa*, Mint family) is another favorite of bees and butterflies. Native to dry thickets, it is a durable plant with excellent growing habits, an ideal showpiece for an informal garden. Bergamot can be found in white, yellow, and lilac as well as the more typical pink. If there is a spot where not much else will grow, or which is too far from the house to be cultivated regularly, a planting of mixed Monardae will solve the problem and present an impressive display in late summer.

TRAILING ARBUTUS or MAYFLOWER (*Epigaea repens*, Heath family) is a borderline recommendation for a wildflower garden because it needs extremely acid soil, pine needles, and painstaking care, but it is worth trying to move this lovely,

fragrant plant into protective custody for already ruthless "pickers" have almost exterminated it in the East. If the delicate Arbutus can be persuaded to respond to your care, it will be a triumph indeed.

WILD BLEEDING HEART (*Dicentra eximia*, Bleeding-heart family) is closely related to Dutchman's-breeches. Its flowers are somewhat the same shape though the color is different. This native of the forests grows as high as two feet, and produces its striking pink flowers all summer long.

BLUE TO PURPLE

HEPATICA (*Hepatica americana*, Buttercup family) is an American native, sometimes called Liverwort because its leaves are vaguely liver-shaped. Its blue, purple, and white flowers appear as early as December on wooded hillsides from Nova Scotia to Florida, and continue blooming until May. It is easy to grow, multiplies freely, and has been known to bloom even under snow.

JACOB'S-LADDER or GREEK VALERIAN (*Polemonium reptans*, Phlox family) is an eastern American variety of the large Phlox family, whose cultivated varieties are a garden staple. It is a small plant, pale blue to lavender in color.

GREAT BLUE LOBELIA (*Lobelia siphilitica*, Lobelia family) is a vivid blue flower that blooms in late summer, when many other flowers have ceased to bloom. It grows almost everywhere in the United States, and, since in many places it has wandered from the woods into the open, it adapts easily to a variety of soil conditions in a garden. Lobeline, an antispasmodic used to treat laryngitis and asthma, derives from Lobelia. Overdoses can be poisonous; children should be warned not to handle this plant.

WILD GERANIUM or CRANE'S-BILL (*Geranium maculatum*, Geranium family) grows profusely, in and out of woods, from Maine to Georgia and in the Far West. It is highly desirable in the garden, not only because its rose-purple flowers have a simple, classic beauty, but because in this one small plant can be found a primer on pollination. The hairs that cover its stems, branches, and calyxes discourage invasion by smooth-bodied insects, which might otherwise crawl up and drain the nectar without being of any use in the dispersal of the pollen. At the base of each petal is a woolly tuft that also serves to protect the nectar. While the anthers are maturing the flower is male, the pistil tightly protected against any chance of self-pollination. Only after enough fuzzy-bodied insects have visited the nectar, and the anthers, denuded of pollen, have dropped, does the pistil unfold and ready its stick stigmas for fertilization. On a sunny day flying insects can alter the Wild Geranium from male to female in a matter of hours.

GREEN TO BROWN

Among the pristine whites, the delicate pastels, and the vivid reds and blues, there is a handful of odd wildflowers that bloom in shades of green to brown—more interesting perhaps than beautiful, but very much worth the gardener's trouble.

JACK-IN-THE-PULPIT (*Arisaema triphyllum*, Calla family) is a curious and appealing plant whose true flowers are almost hidden at the base of its strange hooded "pulpit." In late summer and fall it decorates itself with brilliant red berries. The Jack-in-the-Pulpit is fascinating to botanists because it can perform a peculiar biological trick: It can, and frequently does, completely change its sex. Young plants are almost always male; but in a favorable environment they begin to produce female flowers and eventually, over a period of years, become completely female. Transplanting a female often shocks it into turning male again. Because of this, botanists hypothesize that the key to the metamorphosis lies in the life struggle. The young plant, fighting for food and air, cannot store up enough strength to produce and protect seeds. It remains male, therefore, until it can accumulate strength, and then starts producing female organs. Transplanted, it reverts to the male state, which makes fewer demands on its reserves and allows them to be available for its own survival.

The Jack-in-the-Pulpit is also called Indian Turnip. Its exceedingly bitter corms can be eaten after lengthy boiling, but in the raw state they were so acrid that in some Indian tribes they were used in puberty rites. A young brave could advance toward manhood by showing enough endurance and self-control to eat one.

WILD GINGER (*Asarum canadense*, Birthwort or Knotweed family) bears its dark brown flower underneath the large green leaves. It is not the same as true Ginger Root, which comes from India and is cultivated. However, when the Wild Ginger rhizome is broken open, it gives off a gingery smell. The American Indians drank an aromatic brew of this as a digestive or diuretic.

SKUNK CABBAGE (*Symplocarpus foetidus*, Arum family) is a vegetable-world curiosity that no wildflower garden should be without. However, it must be transplanted into a damp area and by itself, because it was not named by accident. The whole plant, from the purplish-brown spathes (often mistaken for the plant's flowers, which it encloses) to the large, spreading leaves, gives off an unpleasant stench, especially when bruised; and in nature's foolproof plan this is precisely the odor that attracts carrion flies in the very early spring when the Skunk Cabbage blooms. In its growing process, this fascinating oddity generates enough heat to push up through snow, outracing even the Hepatica. Skunk Cabbage is common in the Northeast and on the West Coast. From the evidence of related species in southern Asia and its distribution here, it may have been brought over as a glacial deposit.

As indicated, some of the plants above thrive in damp or swampy spots. Of course, there are others that can be found growing in water, as well as around it. With care, they can be moved to the right kind of habitat—a water garden, or at least a place where they can have perpetually "wet feet."

WATER LILY (*Nymphaea odorata*; Water-lily family) is easy to grow in a pond or lake and makes a magnificent display as its large pink or white flower opens in the morning and closes at night. This variety is an American native, but it is closely related to the venerated Lotus of the Orient, the flower that is idealized in Egyptian art, immortalized in Indian prayer, and believed by the faithful to have carried the Buddha into the world. The Pond Lily is a less majestic relative, but its bright yellow flower makes a lively addition to a water garden.

FORGET-ME-NOT (*Myosotis scorpioides*; Forget-me-not family) is another flower that traces its history back to Egypt, and is the focus of numberless legends. The most famous is that of the German knight who fell into a swift-flowing stream while picking the flower, and had only time to toss it to his lady-love, crying, "Forget me not!" before the current swept him away. The flower's aura of wistful sentimentality made it a special favorite of Victorian lovers, but even a gardener who is not in love can enjoy growing it beside a brook or in a boggy spot.

PICKERELWEED (*Pontederia cordata*; Pickerelweed family) is widely distributed in streams, bogs, and lakes of the eastern

Charming, undated American painting is called "Ample Grove." Love poem at top tells of planting trees. If they fail to grow, poet will never again see his beloved's face.

Red Pine, blossom

White Pine

Blue Spruce, new growth

↓ Apple tree

Maples

Tulip tree, blossom

Witch Hazel

↑ *Dogwood*   ↓ *Hickory*   *Mountain Laurel*

seaboard and Canada. It can be moved into shallow water, where it does best when its roots are anchored in mud. Its strikingly beautiful blue flowers rise from one to four feet above the water.

MARSH MARIGOLD or AMERICAN COWSLIP (*Caltha palustris*, Buttercup family) is another plant to set beside a running brook or in a marshy spot. Its shining deep yellow will give advance notice of spring when there is little other color to be seen.

TREES AND BUSHES

With these flowering plants, and the many others that the gardener will discover for himself, it is possible to make a wildflower garden that will bring endless pleasure. Nature offers even more treasure for the brave; there are trees and shrubs that can be moved out of the wilds and safely set into the right place, at the right time, with the right handling.

It is no easy matter to move a tree. Some are more difficult to transplant than others; but there are general rules that should always be followed. Select a species of tree that is amenable to being moved. Have the new site chosen and the hole dug before you bring the newcomer on the premises. It is hard enough for nurserymen to dig up and re-establish a large tree; do-it-yourself transplanters must always select a small, manageable specimen, and dig widely and deeply enough to avoid damage to the roots.

WHITE PINE (*Pinus strobus*, Pine family), even if planted when small, will be a giant in ten years or less. A row of white pines makes an excellent screen along the roadfront or between houses, and one tree on a front lawn will be a year-round delight.

Maple branch in early spring (top) displays blossoms which soon will fall, strewing ground in pattern of green and gold. Very large old live oak (bottom) grows in dry, sandy soil near coast. It is evergreen.

The dense, rich green needles shelter warblers and finches, and in the forests the pink Lady's-slipper and the yellow Clintonia seem to prefer living at its base. In its distinguished past, the White Pine of New England provided masts and spars for the sailing ships of Britain and America.

HEMLOCK (*Tsuga canadensis*, Pine family) was one of the pleasant discoveries the first settlers made when they began to explore the American wilderness. John Banister, a Church of England minister who became an enthusiastic New World naturalist, sent the first specimen of Northern Hemlock back to England around 1723, along with many other plants that were new to English gardens. The foliage of this hemlock has a particularly attractive color and texture and, by the way, absolutely nothing to do with the potion made famous by Socrates.

MAPLES (*Aceraceae*) of many varieties are found in the American woods. The Indians were producing maple sugar long before white men made an industry of it. Nonetheless, William Hamilton, one of the wealthy amateurs who helped make Philadelphia a horticultural center around 1800, introduced the Norway Maple from Europe to his estate on the Schuylkill River.

So many other deciduous trees can be taken from the forests that the gardener who is prepared to operate with all the necessary knowledge and caution can almost decide what size, shape, and color he wants for a particular location, and then go out and find it. The Ash, Birch, and Locust, for example, can be transplanted when young and grow quite quickly into what city children call "real trees" (apparently those trees whose tops you have to look up to).

SASSAFRAS (*Sassafras albidum*, Laurel

family) is an unusual tree that eventually will grow into a forty- to fifty-foot treasure. Barrels were once made of sassafras wood, and a pleasant tea can be made from the outer bark.

FLOWERING DOGWOOD (*Cornus florida,* Dogwood family) is easy to find but not so easy to transplant; however there is no reason why any wildflower garden should be without specimens of both the pink-flowering and the white. These American dogwoods, spectacular in full early-spring bloom, have equally beautiful relatives in the Old World.

TULIP TREE (*Liriodendron tulipifera,* Magnolia family) is another lovely flowering specimen, which can be established successfully if a very small sapling is selected and care is taken not to break or injure the long tap root. The Tulip Tree sometimes goes by the characterless name of White Poplar, which gives no indication of the remarkable beauty of its large red-and-yellow blossoms. The Dutch settlers, quick to recognize its ornamental value, were growing it in their gardens along the Hudson as early as 1758.

Apple, Cherry, Hickory Nut—all the wild fruit trees—have blossoms, or blossom-like leaf configurations in the spring, and are worth transplanting for the charm they will add to the landscape. The Hickory particularly is a fascinating sight, for its end-leaf unfolds into a flower-like shape of a marvelous pink before it turns green and becomes, recognizably, a leaf.

SHADBUSH (*Amelanchier canadensis*) supposedly received its name because it blooms when the shad are running, but why it is called a bush when it grows into a small tree from twenty to thirty feet high may puzzle the layman. The answer is

Lady Fern, in autumn

↓ Christmas Fern

90

Microphotograph of horsetail stem

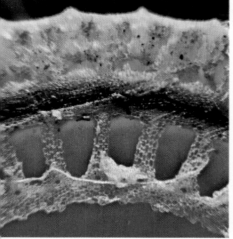

Scouring Rush (horsetail)

Christmas Fern, in spring

91

Interrupted Fern

Maidenhair Fern

strictly botanical: A bush, or shrub, is a woody plant that has more than one stem and produces flowers at, or below, eye level. The Shadbush meets these criteria, no matter how much it looks like a tree.

WITCH HAZEL (*Hamamelis virginiana*), like the Shadbush, straddles the categories of bush and tree—the Witch Hazel is a tree that resembles a bush. The American variety bears bright yellow flowers and, fascinatingly, shoots out its ripe seeds with enough force to send them several feet away. Witch Hazel leaves and bark make a soothing astringent, one of the few ancient cure-alls still in use. Like the English Hazel, its branches were, and perhaps in some places still are, used in water-divining.

MOUNTAIN LAUREL (*Kalmia latifolia*; Evergreen Heath family) is beyond doubt the most useful shrub the gardener will ever find in the American wilds. If he transplanted nothing but healthy laurels his garden would be a showplace. In 1734 the British nurseryman Peter Collinson, who was already specializing in plants imported from the Colonies, wrote to Colonel John Custis in Virginia that, among other specimens, he would be glad to be supplied with "... a sort of Laurell or Bay that bears bunches of Flowers not unlike the Laurus Tinus. . . ." It remained for Peter Kalm, a Finnish pupil of Linnaeus, however, to write such rhapsodies about the American Laurel that Linnaeus named it for him, *Kalmia*. Kalm had been sent by the Swedish government on a botanizing trip through northeastern America that lasted more than three years. His discoveries and specimens were legion, but he was especially enthusiastic about the Laurel: "... when all other trees stand quite naked ... these cheer the woods with their green foliage . . . the flowers are innumerable and sit in great bunches. . . ."

FERNS

There are only one hundred or so ferns in North America compared to the thousands of wildflowers, but they grow almost everywhere, transplant quite easily, and can add a new shape and texture to a garden. This large, complicated family of *Pteridophyta,* has descended almost unchanged from the oldest plants known. They range in size from the tiny, almost moss-like Spleenwort to tropical specimens in South America and the Pacific Islands that reach heights of forty feet.

Cinnamon Fern (*Osmunda cinnamomea*), which comes up in the early Spring, is an unusual reddish-brown color. It begins tightly furled, almost like a small fist, and gradually unwinds as it grows. The Christmas Fern, an evergreen, grows in decorative clumps, fairly easy to find, and derives its name from its use by early settlers as a Christmas green. Other varieties worth seeking are the Interrupted Fern, whose irregular outline results from an alternating arrangement of fertile fronds and sterile pinnules; the American Ostrich Fern, which grows in swampy places to a majestic height, often as tall as a man; and the North American Maidenhair Fern, which like other ferns will grow in moist, heavily shaded places.

Like the fern, the horsetail (*Equisetum*) emerged very early in the long history of plant life. It has no value to the wildflower gardener, for it is far from handsome and difficult to transplant. But its survival, almost unchanged, over the eons speaks of an enormous life force that makes it well worth our notice.

Bunchberry

Pitcher Plant

Bunchberry, close-up

Pitcher Plant flower

In 1848, Asa Gray's *Manual of Botany*, describing the treasure house of "native materials" that had been opened to the rest of the world with the colonization of America, listed 2,067 wildflowers of the Northeastern states. When the eighth edition of the *Manual* was published in 1950, covering the Central states and adjacent Canada, as well, the list stood at 8,340. Adding those that originated elsewhere and those developed by trading, exchange, and natural cross-fertilization, botanists estimate that there are now some 200,000 wild plant species.

Not all of these hide in the protected shade of the woods. In fact, many flourish boldly in the open, because they need light and sun and can manage with soil less rich than natives of the woods and waters. They pattern open fields and meadows with color; they spring up along the roads, beside railroad tracks, in waste places. They are so hardy, persistent, and ubiquitous that they are an instance of familiarity breeding contempt; ruthlessly we uproot and destroy them, refer to most of them as weeds, and never notice how lovely some of them are.

A weed, according to the Oxford Universal Dictionary, is "a herbaceous plant not valued for use or beauty, and usually growing rank...." Applying this to many familiar "weeds" turns out to be very loose talk, indeed. Take, for example, chicory. This stalky plant with its vivid blue flowers makes excellent hay. It roots can be dried, powdered, and used, as they are in Europe, as a coffee substitute. Related to the elegant endive, its leaves are edible, and a variety called witloof is cultivated as a salad delicacy. And some of the earliest love potions known were made from chicory.

Many roadside plants were, and still are, used as food. Even the dandelion, surely the best-known weed of our time, is not entirely without its pleasures. While one householder is ruthlessly digging it out of his lawn and casting it on the rubbish heap, his neighbor may be pulling it up with respect, to break its leaves into a salad, or to use it in an old family recipe for dandelion wine. The clover-like Fenugreek is eaten by modern Egyptians as it was by the ancients. In addition, many weedy plants have medicinal value.

We tend to denigrate the wildflowers that grow in the open. Most of them do not even appear on the conservation lists by which each state's Department of Parks or Agriculture endeavors to protect valued wild plants. To be sure, there are still innumerable oxeye daisies and Queen Anne's lace, but if we continue to pull off wildflower heads as we walk along country roads and yank plants up by the roots, even vigorous spreaders may diminish—an ecological loss for which there is no replacement.

Like other wildflowers, some of the rough, free natives of the fields have been cultivated into more sophisticated garden varieties. Yarrow, which yields an astringent liquid with which Achilles is said to have stanched his wounds (hence its botanical name, *Achillea*), has been elevated to a place in the flower border, in a yellow shade. The star thistle is the ancestor of the bachelor's button, also known as the cornflower.

By far the most important is the wild rose, progenitor of the approximately thirty thousand species of roses grown today. The history of the rose goes back so far that we cannot fill in all the gaps. Long before the

96

Yarrow

Boneset

↑ Grass of Parnassus

↓ Daisies

↑ Meadow Rue   ↓ Yucca

Groundsel

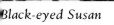

Black-eyed Susan

↑ Buttercups   ↓ Poppies in Mycenae

↑ Wild Rose   ↓ Butterfly Weed

Greeks and Romans assigned it to their gods of love and made it synonymous with all sensuous beauty, the Bronze Age Minoans were immortalizing it on the walls of the House of Frescoes in Knossos. Fossil roses thirty-five million years old have been found in Oregon and Montana. Some form of rose, then, has been known to man from the beginning; and in almost every civilization, it has been considered the queen of flowers.

But it has not merely been venerated; it has been used. Dioscorides and Pliny recommended it in various forms—infusions, tinctures, oils, salves—to cure a list of maladies from superficial irritations to hydrophobia. An early beauty cream was compounded of rose petals and animal fat. Dried rose petals, along with other dried flowers, salts, and spices went into "sweet bags," to perfume airless rooms, exactly as they go into potpourri today for closets and drawers. Rose water, which the Arabs taught the rest of the world to distill, became both a medicinal and a cosmetic staple and still is sold in drugstores. And the rose went from the medieval stillroom into the kitchen with equal facility: dried for flavoring, mixed with flour, sugar, and milk and boiled into puddings; candied as a confection. In the *Herball* of John Gerard, first published in 1597, we find a recipe for rose conserve that "taken in the morning fasting, and last at night, strengthneth the heart," and is also recommended "as well for the vertues and goodnesse in taste, as also for the beautifull colour."

"Take Roses at your pleasure," Gerard continues. "Put them to boyle in faire water, having regard to the quantity...the which you shall boyle at the least three or foure houres, even as you would boile a piece of meat, until they be very tender. Then shall you adde unto one pound of Roses, foure pound of fine sugar...let them boyle gently after the sugar is put therto, continually stirring it with a woodden Spatula untill it be cold." Gerard does not say at what point to remove it from the fire so that it will become cold. The modern cook will use her own judgment.

Despite the high state of development the cultivated rose has reached, a transplanted wild rose still has its own charm, and makes a lovely and co-operative addition to a wildflower garden. The North American species *Rosa carolina* and *Rosa virginiana* are both small, woody plants that transplant well into gravelly soil.

Many other roadside and field flowers transplant easily, and in spite of their "weedy" connotations make surprisingly attractive wildflower plantings. Again, they are arranged by color.

WHITE TO CREAM

OXEYE DAISY (*Chrysanthemum leucanthemum*; Sunflower family) will sometimes move in where it is not wanted, as some of its old colloquial names attest. It has been called Poorland Daisy, Maudlin Daisy, Poverty Weed. But in its cultivated state we call it Marguerite, and there is no reason why the gold-centered white flower should not have a place in the wildflower garden—as long as it is kept in its place and not allowed to straggle. In the Middle Ages a diuretic tea was brewed from its flowers and leaves.

GRASS OF PARNASSUS (*Parnassia glauca*; Saxifrage family) is a lovely little flower which blooms in September in the

Northwest and Middle West. Transplanted into a low moist meadow area, it will bloom when there is little else to be seen.

BONESET (*Eupatorium perfoliatum*, Sunflower family), the white version of the tall-standing Joe-pye Weed, is a native American herb which often was used by Indians and settlers as an emetic and diaphoretic. Another name for it was Agueweed; a concoction made from it was supposed to be effective against shaking fevers or malarial attacks, but it was so nauseatingly bitter that it had to be administered to children with the same degree of force and cajolery as castor oil.

TALL MEADOW RUE (*Thalictrum polygamum*, Buttercup family) and EARLY RUE (*Thalictrum dioicum*) are closely related and follow each other in bloom. Early Rue comes up in moist woods in the spring, Meadow Rue along the roads in summer; both show similar tiny white flowers which sometimes cause them to be mistaken for one another. The Rue of the Bible and of medieval lore is *Ruta graveolens*, a yellow-flowered Eurasian import that grows in American pastures from Vermont to Virginia and has the most interesting history of the three. The strongly aromatic leaves of this plant induce a severe dermatitis in some people. Nevertheless from earliest times they have been used to scent rooms, both to ward off infection and bad odors, and were used in this way in the English law courts until the nineteenth century—along with the traditional nosegay the judge kept in case the close atmosphere threatened to overcome him. Rue had also an intriguing association with chastity, which it was supposed to encourage or protect; when, in *Hamlet*, Ophelia says, "I'll wear my rue with a difference," it is, like the rest of Shakespeare's flower references, no random remark. She is actually offering a clue to one of the many *Hamlet* mysteries—the exact nature of her relationship with the haunted prince.

YELLOW TO ORANGE

GROUNDSEL or RAGWORT (*Senecio aureus*, Sunflower family) is a cosmopolitan plant, well known to the witches of England—it was said—for whom it served in place of broomsticks. In the United States it grows in meadows and along secluded country roadsides, and adds an attractive golden yellow to garden borders or beds through spring and summer.

BLACK-EYED SUSAN (*Rudbeckia serotina*, Sunflower family) is a native American and grows practically everywhere in the country. Almost indestructibly tough, it will survive vicissitudes from man's neglect to abominable weather, and is highly recommended for a garden in which color and gaiety are more important than formality.

BUTTERCUP or CROWFOOT (*Ranunculus bulbosus*, Buttercup family) provides a true test of one's ability to look at the familiar with a fresh eye, for even the wildflower fancier is so accustomed to trampling it underfoot that he may never think of it as a flower. In a grassy garden patch where nothing else will grow he might try planting one of the fifteen hundred varieties of buttercups. They will give him bright bits of color, no matter how poor the soil.

DAY LILY (*Hemerocallis fulva*, Lily family), the familiar bright orange colonizer of roadsides, and the closely related yellow *Hemerocallis flava* were brought from Europe in the sixteenth century as

↑ *Maiden Pink*

Crown Vetch

Musk Mallow

↑ *Lupine*   ↓ *Joe-Pye Weed*

↑ *Vervain*   ↓ *Common Blue Violet*

Blue-eyed Grass

Fireweed

↑ Bluets   ↓ New England Aster

Ironweed

Fringed Gentian wanders
in wet meadows and moist woods,
is not usually found in
the same place twice. Since it
has become rare, do
not pick it, and do not try
to move it. It may
be grown from seeds.

cultivated flowers, but escaped cultivation in many areas and now hobnob with weeds. They are handsome, however, and will add brilliant color to any wildflower garden. Because the Day Lily reproduces vegetatively, spreading freely and sturdily by self-created divisions of its underground stems, some botanists think that all of the millions of Day Lilies in North America may have descended from a single plant.

BUTTERFLY WEED or PLEURISY ROOT (*Asclepias tuberosa;* Milkweed family), an American native, is the most spectacular plant in this color group and the only one on the conservation lists of the many states in which it grows. Its vivid orange-yellow umbels bloom from June through September—when they bloom—for the drawback to transplanting the Butterfly Weed is that under cultivation it does need special attention. Also, it can be transplanted only when very small.

PINK TO RED

DEPTFORD PINK (*Dianthus armeria;* Pink family) is a naturalized American that came originally, like most pinks, from England. Familiar from the time of Chaucer, pinks have been called by many names: gillyflowers, carnations (from coronations), and cloves. The clove gillyflower was much used as a flavoring, particularly in wine and beer—hence also called "sops-in-wine." By the time John Parkinson published his herbal, *Paradisi in Sole,* in 1629, the gillyflower was a garden plant most tenderly cultivated. Parkinson warns that it must only be watered "with such water as hath stood open in the aire...for one whole day at least." The Deptford Pink, however, does not require pampering. Transplanted, it

grows well almost anywhere, even coming into gardens uninvited.

MAIDEN PINK (*Dianthus deltoides;* Pink family) is a decorative pink that makes a wonderful display in a rock garden, especially when combined with other pinks. It is a garden plant in England but has escaped cultivation here.

CROWN VETCH (*Coronilla varia;* Bean family), a native of Eurasia and North Africa, became a cultivated plant in England, but when it was imported into American gardens escaped cultivation and again became a wildflower. It is a tough, coarse plant that spreads far and fast, but if its longitudinal roots are cut or blocked so as to confine it to one area, it will make a beautiful pinkish-lavender patch even in an area where it is hard to grow other flowers.

MUSK MALLOW (*Malva moschata;* Mallow family) comes of a very old family, mentioned in the Bible. American Indians and Mexicans crushed the leaves and roots of this plant to make an emollient juice which they used medicinally. Mixed with salt and honey, it was used to treat fistulas in the eyes and to alleviate the irritation of wasp stings.

FIREWEED (*Epilobium angustifolium;* Sunflower family) is a tall, majestic native American wildflower that would reward more transplanting than it has received. Its name derives from the fact that the plant with its deep pink wands, sometimes eight feet high, often springs up from burnt ground. It also will grow in better environments, and looks handsome against a background of dark green evergreens.

BLUE TO PURPLE

BLUETS, or QUAKER-LADIES (*Hous-*

tonia caerulea; Bedstraw family) is a tiny North American herb that can turn a meadow into a sea of blue. It can be transplanted to create an excellent ground cover or colorful rock-garden tufts.

BLUE-EYED GRASS (*Sisyrinchium campestre*; Iris family) is sometimes also called Fevergrass and Irisette. Each small flower blooms for only one day, but the following day new buds open, and thus Blue-eyed Grass stays in continuous bloom through spring and summer. Since it often is found in meadows with Deptford Pink, one might do well to follow this natural habit and plant the two side by side.

LUPINE (*Lupinus perennis*; Bean family) was recommended by Pliny to aid digestion, and in the eighteenth century it was used in skin care. A cultivated variety comes from Europe, but the slender purple stalks of this species, native to the American Far West and North, are equally graceful.

JOE-PYE WEED, also called Thoroughwort or Queen of the Meadow (*Eupatorium maculatum*; Sunflower family), is found from Quebec to Florida and west to the state of Washington. It is a giant of damp thickets, and its lavender-to-magenta flower clusters—which sometimes are a foot in length—are said to have had curative powers made famous by a New England Indian named Joe Pye, who brewed them into "cures" for a variety of fevers. It goes well with Boneset in moist areas.

BLUE VERVAIN (*Verbena hastata*; Vervain family) has a long historic and probably prehistoric background. It was used as an altar plant and a love philter in Greece and Rome, was sacred to the Nordic god Thor, and was gathered by the Druids "when the dog-star arose from unsunned spots," which suggests that it was one of the ancient plants that had mystical connotations. Gerard, however, dismisses this summarily: "Many odde old wives fables are written of Vervaine tending to witchcraft and sorcery, which you may reade elsewhere ... I am not willing to trouble your ears with such trifles."

BLUE-CURLS (*Trichostema dichotomum*; Mint family) is a small, delicate plant valuable to the wildflower gardener because it flowers in autumn. It is best to grow it from seed, a little extra trouble but worthwhile because the bright blue flowers with their curling stamens are truly charming.

COMMON BLUE VIOLET (*Viola papilionacea*, Violet family) is easily transplanted. It is found with Dandelions in open meadows in early spring, and if set out in congenial locations it will spread without help, turning up as a pleasant surprise in unexpected places, including walks.

NEW YORK IRONWEED (*Vernonia noveboracensis*; Sunflower family) is a North American wildflower whose bushy purple heads are often seen in meadows beside the towering plumes of Goldenrod; the combination is just as effective planted in a garden. (Goldenrod would not be everybody's choice for deliberate inclusion, but it might be simple justice to state that it is no longer considered the prime hay fever culprit; its curse seems to be that it blooms at the same time as ragweed, which *is* guilty.)

NEW ENGLAND ASTER (*Aster novae-angliae*; Sunflower family), in spite of its name, is more common in the South and West than in New England. It looks so much like the cultivated garden aster that it is not always possible to tell whether a meadow specimen is really wild or is one that has

Bladder Campion

Bouncing Be

↑ Bindweed

↓ Queen Anne's Lace

Cheese

Ground Cherry

↑ Golden Alexanders

↓ Devil's-Paintbrush

Burdock

↓ Dandelion

escaped cultivation. The showy purple blossoms can reach eight feet high. It makes an excellent background plant.

SPIDERWORT (*Tradescantia virginiana*; Spiderwort family) grows profusely along roadsides, in gravelly waste places and even between railroad tracks. Its color in the wild is deep blue, but it has been cultivated and can be garden-grown in white and pink. Though it took its Latin name from the famous gardener of Charles I, John Tradescant, Spiderwort is a native of temperate and tropical America.

While many of the field flowers we have discussed are unfairly called weeds, there are others—some handsome, some useful—that cannot really be called anything else, because they have the one unacceptable characteristic that outweighs any virtue: They are uncontrollable. They are the vagabonds among plants. Gardeners and farmers dread them. Their vigorous growth and spreading habits crowd out more delicate, less demanding plants. Following is a list of true weeds so attractive that you may be tempted to domesticate them. Resist the temptation! Pick them if you like (they make effective bouquets), but don't offer them space in your garden, for if you do they will soon be the only plants living there.

WHITE TO CREAM

HEDGE BINDWEED (*Convolvulus sepium*; Morning-glory family) curves its vinelike stem counterclockwise in shrubs, hedgerows, and fences, growing so quickly that it sometimes turns a full circle in two hours. It often comes up beside wild honeysuckle, which curves clockwise, and the ensuing entanglement can be fascinating in a damp, rich meadow but obviously is no

asset to a garden. This cousin of the morning-glory is pleasantly fragrant.

BOUNCING BET or SOAPWORT (*Saponaria officinalis*; Pink family) was brought over by English settlers and is now naturalized in the East and the Middle West. Early New England housewives crushed its leaves and stems in water to make a sudsy solution for washing, but the foam resulting from the saponin content is irritating and may even be poisonous. Therefore, though the pleasant creamy-pink flowers are attractive, this plant should be handled with caution.

BLADDER CAMPION (*Silene cucubalus*) and WHITE CAMPION (*Silene nivea*) are two more members of the Pink family that were brought over from England and now grow wild. The White Campion is particularly attractive, and has an interesting bulging sack from which the petals grow, but, as with the others on this list, it is wiser to go into the fields to admire it than to bring it home.

QUEEN ANNE'S LACE (*Daucus carota*; Parsley family) is the familiar tall, lacy white flower that not only can be seen in almost any field but can easily take the whole field over if left unchecked. The flower is attractive, and the plant can be brewed into a tea that has diuretic, stimulant, and laxative properties, but any virtues it has are negated by its aggressive roots, which tend to choke out surrounding vegetation.

YELLOW TO ORANGE

GOLDEN ALEXANDERS (*Zizia aurea*; Parsley family) has tiny florets of bright golden yellow that appear very early in spring over a large part of the country.

HAWKWEED is a large group of dur-

Milkweed

Heal-All, or Selfheal

↑ Giant Purple Loosestrife   ↓ Scotch Broom

↑ Meadowsweet   ↓ Dogbane

able, vigorous European imports. Its growing habits make it an anathema to farmer and gardener alike. *Hieracium paniculatum*, yellow, and *Hieracium aurantiacum*, orange, are familiar varieties in America in the East and on the Pacific Coast, often growing together in brilliant combination beside a road or in a meadow—where the gardener is advised to leave them. The name Hawkweed stems from a Roman belief that hawks ate these plants to improve their eyesight.

PINK TO RED

COMMON MALLOW (*Malva rotundifolia*, Mallow family) is a modest, inconspicuous plant that often comes up around vegetable gardens and, coincidentally, is edible. Its round, flattish fruit has a nutty, cheese-like flavor with which children in many parts of the world are familiar; they variously call it Cheeses, Pick-cheese, and sometimes Bread-and-cheese. The Hebrews and the Romans ate it as a vegetable, and in some places the leaves still are cooked and eaten. To the French this plant is *Mauve*, which is the shade of its delicate lavender-pink flower.

LADY'S-THUMB (*Polygonum persicaria*, Knotweed family), brought over from Europe, grows almost everywhere in the United States, in dry ground or damp. It has a delicate raceme of tiny pink-to-purple flowers which, like the rest of the plant, are reputed to be diuretic when prepared with boiling water. The plant juices were used for wounds and bruises.

BURDOCK (*Arctium lappa*, Sunflower family) is a six- to eight-foot tall weed whose burry flowers catch in the furry coats of animals and ensure the plant's propagation. In days gone by, children used to weave Burdock seed pods into baskets.

BLUE TO PURPLE

COMMON MILKWEED (*Asclepias syriaca*, Milkweed family) was originally a native of Syria, but grows widely in this country. It has a particularly interesting flower, arranged in such a way that as an insect tries to reach the nectar it tends to slip between the cup-like florets into a sort of trap in which pollen is secreted. Pulling itself free, the insect pulls up pollen bags as well, carrying them along to fertilize another milkweed. The milky juice of the milkweed is allergenic to some people, but young shoots of the plants are said to be as edible and delicate as asparagus. Some species of Milkweed produce pods lined with floss that is usable commercially; during World War II, the floss was discovered to be more buoyant than cork and warmer and lighter than wool, and it became valuable as a lining for life jackets.

HEAL-ALL or SELFHEAL (*Prunella vulgaris*, Mint family) grows all over the world, yet is so sparse that its vivid purple flower is quite unfamiliar, which makes it an atypical weed. In 1653, the herbalist Culpeper wrote: "The juice thereof used with oil of roses to anoint the temples and forehead is very effectual . . ." If there are other reasons for this plant's being called Heal-all, they are lost in history.

VIPER'S BUGLOSS (*Echium vulgare*, Forget-me-not family) is a European immigrant that now grows freely from Quebec to Ontario and southward—too freely for farmers, who consider it an obnoxious pest. A vague resemblance of the bright blue flowers, or possibly of the nuts, to a viper's head led to the name of this plant, and also to its being used in treating snakebite. Medieval herbalists also prescribed it for melancholy; there is no proof that it was effective for either ill.

PURPLE LOOSESTRIFE (*Lythrum salicaria*, Loosestrife family) is a European import. It is cultivated in English gardens, but gets completely out of hand on this side of the Atlantic and is better left in the wild where in late summer it sometimes turns entire meadows reddish-purple.

BOTTLE GENTIAN and FRINGED GENTIAN (*Gentiana andrewsii, Gentiana crinita*, Gentian family) are American natives which sometimes grow in wet woods and swampy places, but are most often found out in the open. They are beautiful in form and color and can be grown from seed. But they are impressive wanderers and unreliable in a garden. The Fringed Gentian in particular is best left alone to grow wherever it has decided to live. Like the Cardinal Flower, the Pitcher Plant, and the Bunchberry it is a treasure which we are more likely to destroy than to preserve if we attempt to move it.

THISTLE (*Cirsium vulgare*, Sunflower family) is an Eurasian plant that found its way to Europe and is now naturalized throughout the United States. It was known, and already feared, in Bible times. The American variety resembles the thistle of Scotland, which, according to legend, achieved its eminence in the eleventh century when Danish invaders, advancing barefoot to surprise a Scottish camp, stepped on the spiny blue flowers and roused the Scots with their shouts of pain.

No sensible gardener would dream of transplanting the weedy wildflowers above, but there is a group of shrubs that can be dug from meadows to add texture, color, and interest to a wildflower garden.

SPREADING DOGBANE (*Apocynum androsaemifolium*, Dogbane family) has no central trunk, but bears its fragrant pink flower clusters on branching stems that grow up to two feet tall. It will do well in neutral or sandy soil. It is adapted for pollination by comparatively strong creatures, such as bees, which can pull themselves loose from a trap-like arrangement at the base of the flower in the nectar bin. The fact that the dogbane is often a death trap for flies and moths should not mar its beauty for the gardener.

MEADOWSWEET (*Spiraea latifolia*, Rose family) prefers damp ground, but its pyramids of lovely pink flowers can also be found on grassy slopes or sterile low ground.

HARDHACK (*Spiraea tomentosa*, Rose family) is a first cousin of Meadowsweet and can be found in the same locations; it grows smaller spikes with deep pink flowers.

SCOTCH BROOM (*Cytisus scoparius*, Pulse family) is a naturalized American plant that was introduced by English settlers, who used it to make a green dye. The Greeks and Romans also had discovered this use for it, and before that, in Bible times, it was eaten: "...and the roots of the broom are their food" (Job 30:4). For medieval herbalists it functioned as a diuretic, a purgative, and, combined with wine, was used for liver troubles. It still appears in the United States Pharmacopoeia, from which most old herbs have disappeared, as a cure for dropsy. Scotch Broom grows along the seashore, and is beautiful on Cape Cod as well as Big Sur. It transplants well into rocky or sandy soil and will cover a slope in spring with a luxuriant show of golden yellow flowers.

7. Composi

The Garden

Designing a garden is like designing anything else that serves human needs and pleasures. The designer must combine a variety of relevant factors to form a pleasing and functional whole. A book, a house, a piece of furniture all share these requirements. And so does a garden, with one important difference. It moves. It breathes, grows, and changes. A juniper that occupies a three-foot circle may, the following year, expand to four feet, thus altering not only its own shape but that of the azalea beside it. An iris that made a clump of purple in just the right place loses color one year and blends drably into the green around it. Weeds take over and rob the rock garden of its tranquil beauty.

The garden designer must meet all the problems of other designers; he must know the space he has to work with and the forms, colors, and relationships of the materials he will put into it; and, because his materials are alive, he must know their habits as well. Yet it is a job an amateur can do if he is willing to learn the fundamentals before putting even one tulip bulb into the ground. Unless the field of operations is acres large and surrounds a mansion, it is possible that he will do better with his own garden than a professional would, because he is involved with a creation that is extremely personal and self-expressive.

Ideally, a garden should be conceived and its broad lines planned before the house it serves is built. But most of us have to contend with a fair list of irreversible facts. If the house is being built, concern with its overwhelming details and problems effectively blocks worry about the garden, and if it is already built, the garden must be

114

H. Cock. excud. 1570.

Opening pages:
English
influence is
evident in
flower bed of
American garden.
Left: "Spring,"
engraving
after Pieter
Brueghel,
the Elder, shows
16th-century
Flemings at
seasonal tasks.

115

Pink Climbing Rose   Yellow Peace Rose   ↓ Iri

Mariposa Lily

116

Pink Rose

↓ Sunflower

Pink

Chrysanthemum

adjusted to the size, mass, and style of the building and the size, outside line, topography, and exposures of the ground available. To some extent topography can be manipulated. Bulldozers can level areas and create small mounds. For the most part, though, the gardener must work with what he has—a vitally important concept, for unless the piece of ground and its potential is known, plants may be added that do not belong in it. And plants probably will not survive, let alone flourish, where they do not belong. Soil, climate, rainfall, wind, sun and shade, surrounding growth—all must be considered. It is useless to visualize six-foot-high rhododendrons across an open area swept by a strong north wind, for example. For the fortunate, they may survive; equally, roses may survive a very damp, heavily shaded spot. But, more likely, they will not, no matter how much cultivation is applied. The trick, as always, is to work with nature, not against it.

Back, then, to the facts of a particular piece of ground. Experts always advise a plan drawn precisely to scale, on graph paper, of the house and its grounds. For some people this works well. Others may find that instead of beginning with such a plan, they do better to take a long look at their grounds from the outside—even from across the road. A little time spent studying the actual house in relation to its ground and its environment can give a much better idea where height and mass are needed, where, for example, a vine or tall shrub will soften a bare corner or screen a bedroom window. The paper plan can follow.

The outside lines should be a first consideration. They can be left to merge freely into surrounding ground or be marked in some way—with a fence, wall, hedge, or border—but a decision should be made before any other planting is done. It is always easier to divide and arrange a space whose outlines are clearly defined. Also, if privacy is desired, it should be planned for at the outset. A partiality to fences should be acknowledged and the property bounded with one at the beginning; otherwise it may later develop that a fence cannot easily be installed because an access gate is required in an impossible place; or perhaps shrubbery has been planted and become well established which would be awkward against a fence. Obviously, the type of fence must conform to the style of the house.

Walks for the predictable flow of traffic to, from, and around the house are the next necessity. With this consider the service needs. Trash must be screened, and if there are small children a play yard is a fine idea no matter how small it must be. A play yard should be planned realistically, that is, landscaped as expendably as possible, so that when the bordering area is trampled on and tricycled over (as it inevitably will be) the destruction will not distress the gardener.

The peculiarities of particular plantings and the needs and services of the household must be taken into consideration, and limit, or at least guide, the over-all plan. For example, a small tree placed near a flagstone path may, in a few years, grow so that its roots may cause the flagstones to buckle and heave. Therefore it is wiser to put the path where it is needed and select a tree whose ultimate growth will not interfere with it—or put the tree farther away. There should also be walks properly placed by flower beds, so that the work of cultivating and the pleasure of picking can be attended to with-

Breathtakingly beautiful spring
tulip beds bloom against
a background of serene, 18th-century
architecture at Williamsburg,
Virginia. Many thousands of plants are
on display, an abundance
few private gardeners can enjoy. Once
past their peak, tulips
must make room for other plantings.

↑ *Tulips in New England*

↓ *Delphiniu*

↑ *Poppy*

↓ *Primrose*

out trampling of the planted area. Walks can be gravel, brick in a variety of patterns, flagstone, crushed marble, expensive polished stone, inexpensive cement—almost anything that is durable, easy to walk on, and pleasing to the eye.

Straight walks are easier to lay out and maintain, but if not carefully designed and sufficiently broad they can give a stiff, unimaginative appearance to a small garden. Curved walks are more graceful, and can make the area seem larger. But the attractive proportions of a curve are by no means as easy to achieve as they may appear to be when encountered and admired in someone else's garden.

On sloping ground the ambitious gardener may undertake a terraced effect, meaning that the path must either slope with the ground's contour or be broken by steps. With their changing patterns of light and shade, well-proportioned steps add interest.

Proportion and scale are key words in the whole of garden design. All the individual components—fence, walks, steps, and eventually the plantings themselves—may be as handsome as money and ingenuity can make them, but they will add up to disaster if they are not in pleasing scale with the house itself, the size of the property, and each other. An overly tall fence will make a small house look like a temporary structure waiting for a permanent building to take its place. If the height is needed for privacy, it might be better achieved with well-placed trees and shrubs.

If time and money restrict outdoor planning to one project at a time, it probably is best to start with a terrace, if the original builder has not provided one. Few builders these days put up houses, even on small plots, without some provision for this kind of indoor-outdoor living; and there are few older houses, no matter what the size, style, or vintage, to which a terrace cannot be added.

A terrace must be placed where it functions well, not merely where it looks best with the house. Most terraces are multipurpose—used for dining, for sunning, for enjoying the air and the view. They should therefore be easily accessible to the kitchen and dining room; be furnished for reasonable comfort; be partly shaded and partly open to the sun; and be sheltered for privacy and yet offer something attractive to look at. While a terrace may appear to be more an architectural than a gardening concern, its needs—shading, privacy, and view, as well as location—can influence the over-all planting plan, and may even control it if the property is small. It is possible to have a large terrace around which most of the horticultural efforts are grouped—in a way, substituting the terrace for a lawn. One large tree may be used to shade the terrace, or masses of evergreen may be used to screen it from the road. A rock garden may be put where it can be seen without moving from a comfortable, shaded chair, or it can be ringed by a perennial border. This is the place, too, for flowering shrubs and plants in large containers. They have been used on terraces throughout recorded time and seem especially to belong there. The material that paves the terrace should be chosen with reference to the material that paves the garden paths. Almost any surface is adaptable as long as it is level enough for chairs to sit squarely, tough enough to be walked upon, and won't be likely to catch the heels and twist the ankles of the unwary.

*Above: Luxuriant plants,
luxuriant lawn, and a small
statue among the verdant shapes.
Far left: Flower bed in
country garden overlaps gravel
walk and shady lawn.
Left: Flowers in front of
fence, a Williamsburg
view and a charming one. Inside,
a small, formal boxwood
garden invites the
stroller to enter.*

123

The gardener also must decide early what kind of atmosphere he desires: formal or informal. "Formal" must be taken loosely; not many of us have the scope or materials that were available to Le Nôtre, and his grand effects have no place or meaning in the average garden scheme. But broad, straight, clean-edged walks, balanced arrangements of trees and shrubs, neatly defined flower beds, and a long, open view will give a more formal effect than, for example, a hillside naturalized with spring-blooming bulbs and, later in the season, day lilies. Freely growing shrubs, a variety of shade-producing trees, curved paths, ground that follows its own natural contours—these elements create informality. For the owner of a typical suburban property this division between formal and informal is far from rigid. An effort at a truly formal garden on an acre or less would certainly look pretentious, while an informal one, if given a really permissive hand, could be disastrous. A gardener should strive for a general mood from the beginning; then each tree, shrub, and group of flowers can be chosen to support it.

Having framed the garden, allowed practicality and circumstances to guide its shape and location, and considered its mood, the gardener has made a fair beginning.

It is likely that even on newly acquired property there will be something to start with: a stripling dogwood, a few forsythia, or, if the gods have been kind, at least one handsome oak, maple, or pine. An old property may even have an oversupply of riches —too many trees fighting for sustenance and light, or, perhaps, a jungle of weedy shrubbery darkening the dining room. The two situations are entirely different, and the problem of eliminating from the old garden is perhaps the more difficult, but there are two cardinal rules that bear on each. The first is not to start until it is clear how and where the garden will end. The second is to evaluate what is already there and build around it.

Every sizable tree is an invaluable asset, and should become a key point in the total design. If more large trees are needed, put them in before other planting is done, and space them so that as they grow they will not encroach upon one another either physically or visually. In general, one really large tree is a better choice than several small ones, but the decision depends very much on the particular piece of ground. Don't let tree hunger, which overcomes most people as they confront a treeless scene, prompt the planting of too many saplings in too small a space. Some authorities insist that each tree should dominate a radius equal to its eventual height. This means that to balance an eighty-foot beech with a forty- or fifty-foot maple, even though the maple is far from mature height when planted, they must be set a minimum of one hundred and twenty feet apart. Since on many lots this would mean no maple at all, even though it might be highly desirable, this guideline should not be regarded as absolute.

In selecting a tree, do not forget its shape and texture as well as its size and mass. An apple tree makes an entirely different pattern from a weeping willow, and a massive pine from a birch. Also, the patterns of deciduous trees are different each season, whereas evergreens fade and thin slightly but give much the same effect the year round.

Using trees as key or control points makes it easier, rather than harder, to arrive at an over-all design. Under a huge shade tree,

124

Roan Mountain Thorn

↓ Holly

126

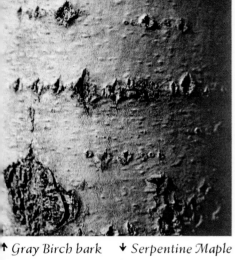

↑ *Gray Birch bark* ↓ *Serpentine Maple* *Pair of hillside oaks*

Espalier-like shape has come naturally to picturesque old maple in middle of fieldstone terrace.

for instance, only certain things will grow, and grass is not one of them. Investigate the shade-accepting ground covers: pachysandra, ivy, periwinkle. If the leaf-and-branch pattern is open enough to let in sunlight, there are plants such as violets, some lilies, and ferns that can be risked. A tree that has an exceptionally handsome shape should be allowed to dominate its area. Treat it as a specimen, and do not distract from its grandeur with shrubs or flowers that would perform better elsewhere.

Smaller trees can be grouped, often with broad-leaved evergreen shrubs. The lines of trees and shrubs should be compatible; for example, a yew of upright habit would battle with the downward-dropping line of a willow, but well-shaped rhododendrons would continue this line so that it began at the ground, rose in a pleasing curve, and

carried the eye downward again.

Flowering trees—dogwood, tulip, chestnut, hawthorn, magnolia—are extremely useful. They add color and texture, and can be used to accent a house entrance, screen the front entrance, or enhance the beauty of a lawn.

Trees must be chosen to fit not merely a design, but site, soil, and exposure conditions. A careful decision is particularly important with trees, because they are expensive investments.

Shrubs also—especially the broad-leaved evergreens—are likely to be permanent parts of the landscape. They can be moved if necessary, but it is less expensive to select a good location in the beginning. The numerous deciduous flowering shrubs can be treated more like flowers, since, like flowers, they perform no landscape function for

128

many months of the year. But evergreens (and this applies even to flowering rhododendrons, for they bloom for only short periods) should be planted where their foliage does the most for your garden. It would be foolish to ignore their flowers completely, of course, but most of the desirable flowering evergreens come in such great variety of colors that selecting a compatible color is no problem. There is one precaution regarding evergreens: Be sure they are evergreens in your climate. Some become semideciduous when exposed to extreme cold.

Even for one devoted to flowers, composing arrangements of non-flowering shrubs can be interesting and diversified. Their foliage and growth habits offer enormous variety and, as for color, "green" can be anything from the almost-gray of some junipers to the almost-black of taxus. It can be the rich gloss of rhododendrons and the feathery spray of hemlock. As a general rule, best results are achieved when strongly contrasting shrubs are not placed in close proximity—in other words, when the contrast is not too abrupt. One strong, dark coniferous shrub can be combined with an evergreen whose leaves are large and smooth, with a few plants whose leaves are small and crisp, like some of the ilexes, and perhaps with a soft-textured plant, like myrtle. A descending scale of leaf size is usually better than an abrupt contrast. This is a reliable guideline to foundation planting around a house, where the primary need is to integrate the house with the ground, and where only a variety of plants can provide the movement for the eye that is essential to accomplish this gracefully. There are places where a uniform massing of shrubs will give a stunning effect, and as

long as they do not march in a stiff regimental line there is no reason why, for example, a stand of mountain laurel should not be set against a section of low stone wall.

Forsythia, brief-flowering and deciduous, is in the vanguard of a whole range of flowering shrubs available to the modern gardener. They have a useful flexibility. Large ones (lilac, weigela, and rose of Sharon are popular examples) can be combined with evergreens, while smaller ones, such as honeysuckle, or those that can be cut back, can be placed in a herbaceous border (herbaceous plants are those that die down to the ground in winter). With the help of a good nurseryman, one can make a selection of shrubs that will keep a border in bloom until fall.

As we have seen, many of the great gardens of the past were green gardens, where flowers were unimportant, where memorable effects were created by impressive trees, shapely shrubs, long vistas, and pavement of formal materials or turf. In many Italian gardens, the small "secret garden"— an outdoor retreat for the women of the house—was the only place where flowers grew in lavish informality. Walking through Williamsburg's marvelous reproductions of seventeenth and eighteenth century English gardens, we understand how much restrained beauty can be created by the individual colors of leaves, the shapes of trees, and their interplay against the sky.

English designers were never quite convinced that flowers had no place in a garden. They had them somewhere around, though they tended to display them in studied, bedded-out arrangements. Toward the end of the nineteenth century a gardener named William Robinson, working at the Botanic

129

130

Top left:
Outstanding specimen
of hawthorn.
Above: Lilac bush,
a charming and
old-fashioned favorite.
Row below, from
left: Clematis, azalea,
rose of Sharon.

131

Garden in Regent's Park, proposed that plants and flowers as they grew in nature would add to formal gardens. His *Wild Garden*, published in 1881, persuaded many gardeners to aim for more natural effects. One of his disciples, Gertrude Jekyll, is generally credited with developing flower gardening into the fine art she believed it could be. In her books and in her own gardens at Munstead Wood in Surrey, Gertrude Jekyll "painted" not only with color but with form. Her feeling that flowers should be combined into living pictures, controlled by the gardener's eye and art, but achieving a more naturalistic beauty than the architectural past had permitted, is shared by every modern homeowner who picks up a trowel and dreams.

Flower beds and borders might be called the punctuation marks of a layout; if they are successful, the exclamation points. Today the old bedded-out style is used mostly by flower-growers, but beds of a freer style can create a delightful effect—possibly the most pleasing for the small, modest garden of a cottage-type house. Luscious color, within a loosely defined outline, strewn across the middle of a lawn or between walks can have a fairy-tale charm. But however spontaneous the "strewing" appears, it must be done with a careful hand. Soft, old-fashioned flowers—pansies, sweet peas, cosmos, and the like—and an artful plan must be combined carefully to arrive at the soft waves of color and continuous bloom that make such a garden.

Most gardeners find it easiest to grow their flowers within a border—the perennial border that has become a hallmark of the Anglo-Saxon gardens of our time. It may include annuals that must be replaced every year, but chiefly it is made up of perennials that require only to be divided, replenished, or moved as space or the whims of the gardener dictate. It is easy enough to have an adequate border. A few simple rules almost guarantee it. Tall specimens should be placed at the back, low ground-hugging ones at the front, and those of medium height in between, so that there is a line of graceful descent from back to front. Plants requiring the same type of soil and exposure should be grouped.

But a border can be more than just adequate. The gardener can truly paint with color, form, texture, line. Plants can be arranged so that pinks, lavenders, blues, and purples run along in neat ribbons of color, or flow into one another in swirling waves; or reds and yellows can punctuate with startling bursts of brilliance. The gardener can plan so that these riches are his from spring through fall. The key word, of course, is *plan*. Buying on impulse can cost a great deal of money, consume time and labor, and achieve a conglomerate jumble in which individually lovely plants muddy each other's colors and forms. Genius, years of experience, or a plan devised by an expert—plus work—are the only foolproof roads to the kind of border of which gardeners dream.

In considering color, the gardener must remember that the basic, ever-present, and most important color in nature is green. Green can be shaped into gardens quite different from those of the grand-mannered past. An all-green woodland or fern garden can be restful and spiritually refreshing. In a world where so much is loud and jarring, the gardener might be wise to create such a refuge, even if it is only a small corner of his property. Without going to such ex-

133

134

*Clockwise from left:
Round cement slabs are
available for
paving paths. Semicircular
brick stairs grace
formal New England garden.
Fieldstone stairway to
studio is edged with
rock-garden planting.
Fountain in flagged
terrace is surrounded
by pots of bright
geraniums. Path is laid
out for leisurely
walks among green and
flowery plantings.*

Top: Down steps, a small sunken bed laid out for easy upkeep. Above: Walks guide traffic. Right: Flagstones harmonize with foundation planting.

136

tremes, green is always present in leaves, stems, grasses. It is the background color against which all other colors are played.

White is the lightest and most ethereal of colors—and the most difficult to find in flowers. Most whites turn out to be slightly tinged with some other color—yellow, pink, and often reflecting green from surrounding foliage. But a garden in pure white (which, of course, is white with green) is worth striving for; it may lack the drama and excitement of a multicolored display, but will offer a clear, pure kind of beauty in its stead. White flowers need not be noble and splendid. Some are delicate and fragile; and some, in addition, yield the loveliest scents in nature, particularly at night. A border might include baby's-breath, daisies, nicotiana, roses, tulips, chrysanthemums, lilies, dahlias, carnations, and the annual petunia. Many of these come in other colors and the white is often forgotten, a mistake, for well-placed clumps of white not only are beautiful on their own but make other colors appear more vivid.

Yellow, the sunshine color—life-giving, life-sustaining, invigorating, gay—should be used with care. Strong shades of yellow, used in combination with pale pinks and blues, may make the delicate colors pallid. Nature provides a profusion of yellow-to-orange flowers, cultivated and wild. Seeing the fresh yellow of the dandelion in a meadow in early spring may make one wonder why we insist on banishing it from our lawns, but there are plenty of other yellows to choose from: chrysanthemums, irises, roses, daisies, yarrow, primroses, violets, tulips, lilies, and the daffodil.

Pink, the irresistible color, charming and romantic, needs thoughtful placement.

Under strong sunlight paler shades can look almost earth-colored. Strong blues and yellows wash out all but the clearest, most vivid of pinks. Like white, it is easily diluted, but a pink and white border is a magical combination, showing both to great advantage. Pinks may be provided by roses, carnations, dahlias, primroses, peonies, rhododendron, laurel, and pinks themselves.

Red is, in one sense, the most foolproof color, for it is so dramatic and vibrant that it leaps to the eye and even when poorly placed cannot help but make an impression. A brilliant red is never lost—it is the colors around it that tend to disappear. Strong, true red is best against green foliage, near no other color, but there are shades of red that combine well with white and true, clear blues; and reds and pinks mixed in a rose garden create a spectacle of the most satisfying richness. Roses alone, of course, offer an enormous variety of reds, and there are so many other reds in cultivated flowers that it seems more useful to point out that it is only with red wildflowers that the choice is limited. In the wild, a true, brilliant red appears only in one wild lily, the cardinal flower, and in bee balm.

Blue, like pink, is romantic, but wistfully and sentimentally romantic rather than sprightly and gay. And clear blue combined with rose-pink is one of the most beautiful combinations a border can display. True blues are considered rare in nature, but if all the blue tones from gray to violet are included and also the lovely herbs like hyssop and lavender, there are enough blues to fill an entire garden (which, incidentally, is not a good idea, for an all-blue garden may be faintly depressing and is not for every taste). Delphiniums come in a wide range of blues, as do the several varieties of bluebells. Then there is spiderwort, both wild and cultivated, lobelia, the innumerable violets and irises, cultivated columbines, bachelor's buttons, verbena, and more.

Purple and lavender create stunning accents. They can be found in lilacs, violets, several kinds of phlox, lupines, clematises, asters, petunias, morning-glories. Like red, strong true purple is best used alone, but the softer lavenders combine well in mixed borders and add richness. To some gardeners purple is the most dignified of colors—perhaps because of its long history as the imperial color of ancient dynasties.

Green is not the only constant color factor with which all these other colors must combine. Blue is almost as pervasive—the blue of the sky against which the colors will be seen, possibly the blue of distant water.

Any color is controlled by the light that falls upon it. As light withdraws, colors change. White turns almost green; purple appears quite brown when the sun no longer strikes it; some pinks look yellow; some reds almost black.

The gardener may prefer to juggle the problems of garden design by himself, to arrive at a truly personal solution—but this is not necessary. He can seek advice from a landscape designer or a nurseryman; or he can turn to libraries, state agricultural stations, and garden clubs. Botanical gardens and arboretums will supply him with pamphlets, professionals eager to keep him from making mistakes, and wonderful gardens on which to train both judgment and eye. He can imitate what he sees, or absorb it and go on to create of his work, his knowledge, his vision, and his taste something that is entirely his own.

COMMON & LATIN NAMES	COLOR & PERIOD OF BLOOM	SUN	HALF-SHADE	SHADE	FRAGRANT	WET	DRY	ROCK GARDEN	HEIGHT IN FEET (1–7)
Hollyhock, *Althea rosea**‡	W, Y, P July-Aug.	X							to 7+
Plume Poppy, *Bocconia cordata*	W July	X							to 7
Swamp Rose, *Hibiscus*, var. Meehan's Mallow Marvels	W, P Aug.-Oct.	X							to 5
Henry's Lily, *Lilium henryi*‡	R Aug.-Sept.	X							to 5
Larkspur, *Delphinium*	B, L, PU June-Oct.	X							to 5
Red Sneezeweed, *Helenium autumnale*, var. Rubrum	O July-Aug.	X							to 4
Giant Daisy, *Chrysanthemum uliginosum*	W Aug.-Sept.	X							to 4
Sneezeweed, *Helenium autumnale*, var. Superbum	O Aug.-Sept.	X							to 4
New England Aster, *Aster Novae-Angliae*	L, P Sept.-Oct.	X					X		to 4
New York Aster, *Aster Novi-Belgii*	P, L Sept.-Oct.	X					X		to 4
Beardtongue, *Penstemon barbatus*†	P June-July	X							to 3
Turk's-Cap-Lily, *Lilium superbum*‡	R June-July	X	X						to 4
Tiger Lily, *Lilium tigrinum*‡	O July-Aug.	X	X						to 3
Bugloss, *Anchusa italica*, var. Dropmore*†	B May-July	X							to 3
Bugloss, *Anchusa italica*, var. Opal*‡	B May-July	X							to 3
Lupine, *Lupinus polyphyllus*	W May-June	X					X		to 3
Chinese Peony, *Paeonia* (albiflora hybrids)	W, P May-June	X							to 3
Blue Sage, *Salvia azurea*, var. Grandiflora	B Aug.-Sept.	X	X						to 3
Meadowsweet, *Spirea lobata*, var. Venusta†	P July-Aug.	X	X			X			to 3
Pink Meadow Rue, *Thalictrum aquilegifolium roseum*†	P May-July	X	X						to 3
Golden-spurred Columbine, *Aquilegia chrysantha*	Y May-Aug.	X	X						to 3
Oxeye, *Heliopsis pitcheriana*	O July-Aug.	X					X		to 3
Gold-banded Lily, *Lilium auratum**‡	W July-Aug.	X	X		X				to 3
Madonna Lily, *Lilium candidum*†	W June-July	X			X				to 3
False Indigo, *Baptisia australis*	B June	X							to 3
Bellflower, *Campanula latifolia*†	L May-July	X	X						to 3
Canterbury-Bells, *Campanula medium**†	L, W June-July	X	X						to 3

How to Use This Chart

The original on which this chart is based was hand-lettered by an unknown—though certainly a dedicated – gardener. It is a remarkable guide to composing a garden in any particular location. Starting with some idea of what he wants to achieve, the gardener can choose at a glance plants that will give the desired effects of color, mass, fragrance, and succession of bloom. A reference to the columns showing the plants' requirements of soil, moisture, and light will confirm their suitability to his plan. Flowers are listed in order of highest-growing to lowest, the order in which they usually are set out. Taller flowers stand at the back of a bed, or in the center of one that is designed to be walked around; in an informal border they can be interspersed with lower ones.

KEY: * Not strictly a perennial   † Holds presentable foliage after blooming   ‡ Foliage disappears or becomes unsightly after plant blooms

COLOR KEY: W-White, P-Pink, R-Red, Y-Yellow, O-Orange, L-Lavender, PU-Purple, B-Blue

Perennials

COMMON & LATIN NAMES	COLOR & PERIOD OF BLOOM	SUN	HALF-SHADE	SHADE	FRAGRANT	WET	DRY	ROCK GARDEN	1	2	3	4	5	6	7
Knapweed, *Centaurea macrocephala†*	O July-Aug.	■							■	■					
Shrubby Clematis, *Clematis davidiana*	P Aug.-Sept.	■			■				■	■	■				
Larkspur, *Delphinium cheilanthum†*	B June-Oct.	■							■	■	■				
Oriental Larkspur, *Delphinium formosum†*	L June-Oct.	■							■	■	■				
Foxglove, *Digitalis purpurea*	W, PU June-July	■	■						■	■	■				
Purple Coneflower, *Echinacea purpurea*	PU July-Oct.	■					■		■	■	■				
Japanese Iris, *Iris kaempferi†*	W, L, PU June-July	■				■			■	■	■				
Japanese Lily, *Lilium speciosum‡*	W, P Aug.-Sept.	■	■						■	■	■				
Rose Loosestrife, *Lythrum salicaria*	W July-Aug.	■							■	■	■				
Blazing Star, *Tritonia crocosmaeflora**	R, O July-Sept.	■							■	■	■				
Hardy Phlox, *Phlox paniculata*	W, P June-Sept.	■							■	■	■				
False Dragon's-Head, *Physostegia virginiana*	W July-Aug., L Aug.-Sept.	■	■						■	■	■				
Garden Heliotrope, *Valeriana officinalis†*	P June-July	■	■		■				■	■	■				
Japanese Windflower, *Anemone japonica*	P Sept.-Oct.	■	■						■	■	■				
Leopard's-Bane, *Doronicum plantagineum‡*	O April-May	■	■						■	■					
Baby's-Breath, *Gypsophila paniculata*	P July-Aug.	■							■	■	■				
Sneezeweed, *Helenium hoopesii†*	O May-June	■							■	■					
Day Lily, *Hemerocallis aurantiaca, H. flava*	O, Y May-June	■	■	■			■	■	■	■	■				
Siberian Iris, *Iris siberica*	W, L, PU May-June	■	■						■	■	■				
Oriental Poppy, *Papaver orientale‡*	W, P May-July	■							■	■					
Common European Columbine, *Aquilegia vulgaris*	W May-June	■					■	■	■	■					
Michaelmas Daisy, *Aster grandiflorus*	L Sept.-Oct.	■							■	■	■				
Hardy Chrysanthemum, *Chrysanthemum*	W, Y, O Sept.-Oct.	■							■	■	■				
Ground Clematis, *Clematis recta*	W June-Aug.	■			■				■	■	■				
Gas Plant, *Dictamnus fraxinella*	W June-July	■	■		■				■	■	■				
Yellow Foxglove, *Digitalis ambigua†*	Y June-July	■	■						■	■	■				
Yellow Day Lily, *Hemerocallis middendorffii*	Y, R June-July	■	■						■	■	■				
German Iris, *Iris germanica‡*	W, B, L May-June	■					■		■	■	■				
Old-Fashioned Early Peony, *Paeonia officinalis*	P May-June	■					■		■	■	■				
Balloonflower, *Platycodon grandiflorum*	L, W July-Sept.	■							■	■	■				
Coneflower, *Rudbeckia speciosa*	Y July-Aug.	■							■	■	■				
Meadowsweet, *Spiraea billiardi*	P July-Aug.		■		■	■			■	■	■				
Turtlehead, *Chelone lyoni*	L Aug.-Oct.		■			■			■	■	■				
Loosestrife, *Lysimachia clethroides‡*	W June-Aug.		■			■			■	■	■				
Rosy Milfoil, *Achillea millefolium, var. roseum*	P July-Sept.	■							■	■					

139

COMMON & LATIN NAMES	COLOR & PERIOD OF BLOOM	SUN	HALF-SHADE	SHADE	FRAGRANT	WET	DRY	ROCK GARDEN	1	2	3	4	5	6
Double Sneezewort, *Achillea ptarmica*	W May-Oct.	■				■			■	■				
Golden Marguerite, *Anthemis tinctoria*	O June-Sept.	■					■		■	■				
St. Bruno's Lily, *Paradisea liliastrum*‡	W May-June	■	■					■	■	■				
Butterfly Weed, *Asclepias tuberosa*‡	R July-Aug.	■					■		■	■				
Peach-Leaf Campanula, *Campanula persicifolia*†	L, W June-July	■	■						■	■				
Coreopsis, *Coreopsis lanceolata*	O June-Aug.	■							■	■				
Bleeding Heart, *Dicentra spectabilis*‡	P April-June		■						■	■				
Blanketflower, *Gaillardia aristata*	O & R June-Oct.	■					■		■					
Cardinal Flower, *Lobelia cardinalis*†	R July-Aug.		■			■			■	■				
Early-flowering Phlox, *Phlox suffructicosa*	W, L, PU June-Oct.	■							■					
Jacob's-Ladder, *Polemonium caeruleum*	B May-July		■						■	■				
Speedwell, *Veronica longifolia*	L July-Sept.	■							■	■				
Mountain Bluet, *Centaurea montana*	L June-Aug.	■							■					
Mistflower, *Eupatorium coelestinum*	B Sept.-Oct.	■							■					
St.-John's-Wort, *Hypericum moserianum*	O June-Aug.	■							■					
Evening Primrose, *Oenothera fruticosa*	Y June-July	■				■	■		■					
Bluebonnet, *Scabiosa caucasica*	L June-Sept.	■							■	■				
Sea-Lavender, *Statice latifolium*†	L July-Aug.	■					■		■					
Dwarf Starwort, *Aster ptarmicoides*	W July-Aug.	■					■		■					
Clustered Bellflower, *Campanula glomerata*†	PU June-July	■							■					
Shasta Daisy, *Chrysanthemum maximum*	W June, July, Oct.	■							■	■				
Lily, *Lilium pumilum*‡	O June-July	■							■	■				
Siberian Coral Lily, *Lilium tenuifolium*‡	P June	■							■	■				
Flax, *Linum perenne*	B May-July	■					■		■	■				
Dwarf Balloonflower, *Platycodon mariesii*	W, L July-Sept.	■	■						■					
Japanese Primrose, *Primula japonica*†	W, P May-July		■	■		■			■	■				
Pyrethrum, *Pyrethrum hybridum*	W, P June-July	■	■						■	■				
Stonecrop, *Sedum spectabile*	P Aug.-Sept.	■					■		■					
Stokes' Aster, *Stokesia laevis*	B July-Oct.	■							■					
Globeflower, *Trollius europaeus*‡	Y May-June	■	■			■			■	■				
Snowdrop Windflower, *Anemone sylvestris*	P April-June	■	■						■					
Rocky Mountain Columbine, *Aquilegia caerulea**‡	L May-June	■	■						■	■				
Sweet William, *Dianthus barbatus**†	W, P May-June	■					■		■	■				
Peony, *Paeonia tenuifolia*‡	P May	■							■	■				
Meadowsweet, *Spiraea astilboides*	W June	■				■			■	■				

KEY: * Not strictly a perennial   † Holds presentable foliage after blooming   ‡ Foliage disappears or becomes unsightly after plant blooms

COLOR KEY: W-White, P-Pink, R-Red, Y-Yellow, O-Orange, L-Lavender, PU-Purple, B-Blue

COMMON & LATIN NAMES	COLOR & PERIOD OF BLOOM	SUN	HALF-SHADE	SHADE	FRAGRANT	WET	DRY	ROCK GARDEN	1	2	3	4	5	6	7
German Catchfly, *Lychnis viscaria*†	P June	■					■	■	■	■					
Bird's-Eye, *Adonis vernalis*‡	O April-May	■	■					■	■						
Avens, *Geum heldreichii*	O May-June	■						■	■						
Coral-Bells, *Heuchera sanguinea*	P May-Sept.	■						■	■						
Iceland Poppy, *Papaver nudicaule**	W, Y, O April-Sept.	■						■	■						
Wild Sweet William, *Phlox divaricata*	P May	■	■					■	■						
Dwarf Jacob's Ladder, *Polemonium humile*	W June-July		■				■	■	■						
Goldentuft, *Alyssum saxatile*	O April-May	■					■	■	■						
Poppy Mallow, *Callirhoe involucrata*	P July-Oct.	■					■	■	■						
Bluebells of Scotland, *Campanula rotundifolia*†	PU June-Aug.	■					■	■	■						
Hardy Candytuft, *Iberis sempervirens*	W April-May	■					■	■	■						
Woolly Yarrow, *Achillea tomentosa*	O June-July	■					■	■	■						
Carpathian Harebell, *Campanula carpatica*	PU, W June-Oct.	■						■	■						
Carnation, *Dianthus latifolius*	P June-July	■					■	■	■						
Grass Pink, *Dianthus plumarius*	W, P May-June	■			■		■	■	■						
Mountain Pink, *Phlox subulata*	R, W, L, PU April-May	■					■	■	■						
Leadwort, *Plumbago larpentae*	L Aug.-Oct.	■					■	■	■						
Siebold's Primrose, *Primula sieboldii*	W, L, PU April-May		■	■				■	■						
Polyanthus, *Primula polyantha*	W, Y April-May		■	■				■	■						
Giant Cowslip, *Primula veris superba*	Y April-May		■	■				■	■						
Hoary Speedwell, *Veronica incana*	L July-Aug.	■						■	■						
Lily-of-the-Valley, *Convallaria majalis*	W May		■	■	■			■	■						
Garland Flower, *Daphne cneorum*	P April-May	■			■			■	■						
Forget-Me-Not, *Myosotis palustris*	B May-Sept.	■	■			■		■	■						
White Rock Cress, *Arabis albida*	W April-May	■					■		■						
Bugle, *Ajuga reptans*	L May-June	■	■				■		■						
Thrift, *Armeria maritima*	P May-June	■					■	■	■						
Mouse-Eared Chickweed, *Cerastium tomentosum*	W May-June	■					■	■	■						
Dwarf Iris, *Iris pumila*‡	PU, Y, W, L April-May	■					■	■	■						
Tunica, *Tunica saxifraga*	P June-Aug.	■					■	■	■						
English Daisy, *Bellis perennis*‡	P April-June	■						■	■						
Dropwort, *Spiraea filipendula*	Y June	■			■			■	■						
Chalk Plant, *Gypsophila repens*	W June-July	■					■	■	■						
Rock Speedwell, *Veronica rupestris*	PU May-June	■					■	■	■						
Tufted Pansy, *Viola cornuta*	B April-Oct.	■	■		■			■	■						

8. In Wild ar

ony Ground

The imaginative gardener can turn a bit of ground that presents a special problem into a special delight. A stony, unpromising bank becomes a rock garden; a low-lying corner, becomes a private wildflower preserve.

One of the happiest ways of gardening is with stones and rocks. To combine a harsh outcropping of inert material with living, moving foliage and to embroider it with tufts and threads of color satisfies a peculiarly creative impulse.

Rocks themselves can have a sculptural beauty. They show fissures and planes; they change with the light of day; they glisten in the moonlight. There is something awesome about them—they remind us of what is concealed, and like the tips of icebergs put us in momentary touch with the hidden forces that shape and reshape our earth. Plants curling and curving and reaching out against these unyielding surfaces are all the more appealing for the contrast; their colors, spangled against cold grays and browns, all the more exciting. Pinks and phlox, irises, the dwarf rhododendron, veronica, Virginia bluebells, dame's rocket, trillium—there are dozens of varicolored blooms to turn a rock garden into a jewel box, more than repaying the work that must precede the reward.

Actually, the lazy gardener may be better off with a rock garden than with one that involves lawns, beds, and borders. The planning takes work, for it must be either inspired or painstaking; and as the average gardener cannot look at a shady patch and compose it with an artist's eye into a vision of beauty, he must be prepared to take infinite pains to achieve his beautiful garden. Once the design is set and the rocks are in place, the upkeep is not staggering—a small amount of weeding, feeding, and replacing of material and the rocky enclave is alive with color for months. Stones reflect heat and sunshine more than earth, so that many rock garden plants begin to bloom in early spring before much else is stirring. If some plants are to be collected from the woodlands, it will be well to go out very early in the year and find the dazzling white of the saxifrage thrusting out of rock fissures, and anemones and bloodroot blooming in stony ground. With a good placement of low evergreens a rock garden will be a pleasure to look at even through a window closed against the winter.

What we usually think of as a rock garden —a sloping area tightly planted and bursting with color between well-arranged rocks— started out as an English specialty. It was Francis Bacon who wondered in print, somewhat wistfully, why the Elizabethan greensward couldn't be varied with "little gardens of irregular hillocks planted with wild strawberries and the other herbage of copse and hedgerow." Somebody added rocks, and subsequent generations of English gardeners set their hillsides and stone walls blooming with greenery and color. By the nineteenth century the rock garden was a formal, deliberately styled adjunct to manor-house gardens, often a showcase for rare plants collected in odd parts of the world by men who could afford to travel, or at least to pay for what traveling professionals brought back. At one time a nursery in Geneva offered seven thousand kinds of rock plants for sale. Rock gardening became a hobby as passionately pursued as memoir writing and stamp collecting.

The influence of the "classical" English

Preceding pages: Panoramic view of rock garden planned with care and skill. Opposite: Blue veronica, with azalea, basket-of-gold in distance.

144

rock garden is apparent in America from coast to coast, though the content varies with the climate. The high, hilly northwestern states are famous for displays that include the desirable alpine plants, which gardeners in lower, warmer regions must resign themselves to doing without. There are other memorable rock gardens on the West Coast—the Botanical Garden in Claremont, California, and the Strybing Arboretum in San Francisco have exceptional examples. The massive granite outcroppings of the New England states also lend themselves to spectacular planting. The lovely natural area on Mount Washington in New Hampshire has been further beautified by landscaping art and is now an alpine garden of special beauty.

With the end of World War II, America discovered Japanese food, Japanese architecture, and, with a dozen other aspects of an unfamiliar way of life, the Japanese rock garden. This was not a new kind of garden design. For many centuries before Francis Bacon's "little hillocks" the Japanese had been combining stone with plant material to create areas of philosophical and spiritual significance as well as of physical beauty. Even in purely decorative Japanese gardens the eye is teased and the imagination stimulated. A natural scene may be re-created in miniature. A scattering of polished stones between shrubs represents a stream; a group of rocks is composed to suggest a waterfall, a slab on its side becomes a bridge. In the temple gardens rocks may be arranged with ritual significance. A grouping on a hillside in the Saihoji Temple garden symbolizes the obstructions that must be surmounted on the way toward an understanding of Zen Buddhism. In the famous garden of the Ryoanji Temple, faithfully reproduced at Brooklyn (N.Y.) Botanical Garden, sand is rake-patterned around a composition of fif-

*Left: Natural garden in which
rocks themselves are used for planting.
Above: Unusual but effective—and
neighborly—rock garden beside road
is planted with pinks, irises, and
snow-on-the-mountain.*

147

148

Three photographs
portray varieties of
garden pinks,
a family known in
one form or
another
since Theophrastus.
Page from Paradisi
in Sole contains
other English species.

149

teen rocks to suggest the sea lapping at islands. There are no plants, no living green; nothing to distract from the rhythmic serenity which is meant to lead the observer's thoughts away from the material world to the contemplation of abstractions.

The esoteric symbolism of oriental garden art cannot really be transplanted into a western atmosphere, but we have only to look around any suburb, particularly at contemporary houses, to see that the feeling and style of Japanese gardens have been imitated to the point of faddism. Most likely, this will subside; meanwhile, from their adaptations, Americans are learning useful lessons. Harmony between elements and site, good proportion, a reverence for natural forces are important in Japanese design but not peculiar to it; they have been as important in the West, though interpreted differently and with different materials. To combine a dwarf laceleaf maple with a single dramatic rock, and set them in a pool of white pebbles instead of in a fluttering riot of mixed annuals, takes a new kind of eye. More and more, gardens demonstrate an understanding of the value of spareness, the meaning of pure form, the importance of balancing space and mass. Simplicity of form and purity of shape can have enormous appeal—particularly in a time when much that comprises people's lives, what they see and think about and cope with each day, is a convulsive state of complication. Should gardeners, in effect, compound the confusion by choking more and more plants into less and less space, or rather create havens of serenity and refreshment for eye and spirit?

A rock garden is a combination of rocks with plants. It does not require a hillside, or even a bank. It can be made on a flat piece of land, in a bit of private woodland, in the middle of a lawn-and-border garden, in a desert, on a beach. Anywhere, as long as two things are kept in mind. Try to use native stone or rock, and be sure that it is appropriate to the garden area. If there are not enough appropriate stones, garden stone can be bought from lumberyards, building suppliers, and nurseries, but it will not take root, so to speak, unless it suits the area. A piece of clean, raw quarried stone, whose surfaces have not been exposed, will be an ungainly interloper in a verdant spot. Here a rock is needed that looks as if it had been grained and darkened by weather, tossed around in turbulent waters, stained by burial in the earth. The cleanly glistening rock, on the other hand, will thrust up from a seaside rock garden like a piece of elemental sculpture.

Rocks will probably have to be moved into your domain or at least moved within it. (A small truck-hoist can be hired to facilitate this.) As the eye is trained, geological misfits will become glaringly apparent. In general, round stones do not assemble as well as flatter ones; the latter are also easier to move, and encourage small creeping plants, like the innumerable and invaluable sedums, to grow over them and into cracks, thus relating the whole composition to the ground. In placing rocks, choose the flattest surface of even a rounded rock for exposure. Try for variety in size and in spacing. Wads of crumpled newspaper can serve as standins to suggest how the rocks will look while locations are being pinpointed.

As with plants, so with rock: More is not necessarily better. Three parts plant material to two parts rocks is a rule some experts follow. Like any rule of thumb, it is only a

150

guide, to be bent to the gardener's own site and taste.

The rule has no application at all in a naturally stony area. Often the earth's geological unrest has exposed a grouping of stones that collect their own plant communities. Mosses and lichens settle in the fissures and spread over the surfaces; ferns root in damp shade between the masses. It would be a gross error of taste to interfere with nature's arrangements here. Soft, pretty garden flowers would be lost, and diminish the grandeur of the rocks. Instead, bring in more small, wild, creeping things, add sword ferns for contrast.

Interesting gardens can also be made of the stony debris called scree. This is stone, flaked or chipped by ice, water run-off, and other natural processes, which collects in deep layers at the base of cliffs and in other mountain spots where leaves do not form a ground cover and topsoil does not accumulate. The plants that grow in scree are true rock plants, whose tough, cord-like roots draw enough nourishment from a harsh environment to make them desirable and reliable in any kind of rock garden. Nature's harmonies are always the most satisfactory when they can be duplicated, and thus these plants look and flourish best in the environment from which they came—scree that is created, or re-created, in the garden. Think of it as an alternative to green ground cover, in the spaces between plants and rocks, and its possibilities will be apparent.

To establish a good scree, loose enough for drainage yet dense enough to be decorative, fill a foot-deep foundation with a mixture of sand, gravel, and a little soil. Spread over the surface crushed stone of any color that blends with the native rocks

Artist of school of early 17th-century Mogul emperor Jahangir depicts graceful iris as attracting small birds.

151

*Above: Flower-laden
landscape in
Montana. Right: Dwarf
azalea grows beyond timber
line. Edelweiss is
mountain climber's badge
of courage. Opposite:
Alpine poppies (top)
of American West.
Kidney vetch
(bottom) is cultivated
in Belvedere Palace
garden in Vienna.*

153

Goldthread
(above)
and pyxies

154

nearby, bluestone, or the elegant and expensive white pebbles that are available in several sizes. With plenty of sun and constant replenishment of the water supply, many varieties of juniper and euonymus will do well in scree, as will dwarf alpines.

A stone wall can also be a rock garden, a special kind with intriguing possibilities when space and the gardener's time are limited. Nature sometimes creates one singlehandedly. One of the most charming of country-life surprises is to ramble past a neglected bit of retaining wall and find that it is in full bloom. Mosses have appeared through no human agency; sedum planted nearby has crept into cracks and begun to bloom; ivy vines and ajuga have ventured out on their own from some planting in the vicinity and established new outposts between the old wall's loosely laid stones. Christmas ferns and polypody are particularly welcome invaders, for once set in spots of their own choosing they grow and spread rapidly.

But if nature has not offered this miracle, it is not difficult to create. In a loosely laid "dry wall"—one not held together by mortar or cement—earth mixed with a small amount of leaf mold or peat will easily hold the roots of small plants and produce, before too long, a marvel of blooming plants amidst the stone. Any small fern that is not particularly sensitive to the sun, any sedum, many vines, and the ubiquitous "hen-and-chickens" (*Sempervivum soboliferum*) will take happily to vertical growth. On the steeply sloping streets of cities like Seattle, necessity has been the mother of much beauty. Miles of retaining walls, built to preserve the contours of the land, burgeon with vines and rock plants that conceal the stonework.

A walk can be a variant of the rock garden. The slope leading to it, its edges, the cracks between stones can be set abloom with tiny plants. A time-honored trick of herb fanciers is to plant thyme between paving stones; pressed underfoot, the small, tightly bunched leaves release their spicy scent into the summer air. Heather (*Erica*), whose story goes back to the Bible, can be grown from seed and is also charming between stones in a walk, though it need not be confined there. There are approximately thirty cultivated varieties available in the United States whose delicate shades of white, pink, and lavender combine beautifully with other flowers in any rock garden.

As with many aspects of gardening, from the best kind of compost to the formulas guaranteed to produce perfect proportion, a whole mystique has grown up around alpine plants, ruled by those who claim to have unlocked special secrets. An alpine garden is simply a rock garden in which plants from high elevations will flourish. That is why Washington, Oregon, Maine, and New Hampshire can boast of magnificent alpine displays, why gardeners in the middle belt of the United States can manage them only with great patience and extra care, and why a southern gardener can attempt them only as an experiment, a challenge, or in an alpine greenhouse.

From the Himalayas to the Alps and the Rockies, the vast alpine ranges of the world are seas of indomitable plants, spread by wind, by rain, by ice in the crags and crevasses, by scree as it moves to the urging of the elements. The vegetation that survives above the tree line has adapted itself in highly specialized ways. Because they must be more toughly rooted, stronger, and more vigorous than lowland plants, small flowering alpines tend to produce more brilliant color. Alpine conifers, twisted and gnarled by their struggle with the elements, grow in grotesquely fascinating shapes, which have been used and imitated for generations by the Japanese in their miniature bonsai gardens. Since commercial diggers made these stark, distorted pines and hemlocks widely available about twenty years ago, they have been used dramatically against contemporary houses. Over-use, however, has somewhat dimmed their dramatic impact, and as they adapt to more moderate climates, their habits change—their angles become covered by heavier growth and they begin to resemble the pines and hemlocks indigenous to lower altitudes.

Alpine gardens are collectors' showplaces, and while not even a rabid collector is likely to climb above the timberline to gather his own alpine trees, ideally the more distinctive portable plants should be gathered personally. Many small alpines of proven adaptability now are commercially available. Travelers returning from the Swiss and Austrian Alps used to boast of having climbed so high they saw the edelweiss in flower; now seed of this once-elusive native of the high crags is sold by many nurseries that specialize in alpines. Provided with mountain soil, usually acid, and plenty of water, it does well in rock gardens far below its original habitat. Many of the varieties of gentians that can now be grown from seed were originally alpine plants. To bring these wild plants down to earth successfully takes know-how, special equipment, and care, and the unprepared amateur may as well stay below. The expert knows which of the small alpines will survive hours

Rock garden planted with heather. Below: Close-up of heather in Scotland.

in a rucksack, and how the roots must be packed in moist moss or earth and encased in plastic or aluminum foil to retain the moisture. In this manner some wild mountain cyclamen have been brought down successfully, as have dwarf azaleas and mountain goldenrod, which is richer in color and more abundant in growth than the field variety. Sometimes these flowers, like the conifers change slightly as they adapt. A tough mountain fighter may lose some of its vigor or color in its new, less demanding home. But to the collector who considers "You can't grow that down here!" a challenge, this is a small price to pay for the achievement of keeping the plant alive.

All sorts of challenges remain above the timberline. Some day an undefeatable plant adventurer may even bring down the alpine rose, which grows at such high altitudes in Austria and Switzerland that to some it is almost a legend. It has not been acclimatized in the United States, but it might be someday, for the alpines that adapt most successfully are often close relatives of plants long-established below—and the alpine rose is a member of the rhododendron family.

Besides providing a suitable climate, the gardener must reproduce as much of the original habitat as possible: the constant sun on the high slopes, the type of rock, scree, or soil the plant is used to, even the plants that in nature grow alongside it. And what is necessary for alpine plants is equally necessary for any wild plant. Anyone interested in creating a wildflower garden of any kind, bringing into his private preserve native plants of the forest, fields, desert, or swamp, first must undertake to study the plants' original environments.

156

Heather garden among rocks on edge of lake is very effective.

158

An appreciation of the wild, stubborn plants that spring up along the roadsides or the shy ones that grow in hidden places is sufficient reason to make a garden of them. However, there is another very good reason. The successful wildflower gardener is a conservationist, helping to preserve life which might otherwise succumb to the bulldozer and the asphalt spreader. That is why, while it is important for cultivated flowers to be planted in compatible environments, it is especially important for wildflowers. If a gardener plants a Rubaiyat rose and it dies, any nursery can sell him a replacement, but if he digs up a wild wood lily and then kills it by planting it in the wrong place, he may have a hard time finding another.

How does one work with wildflowers with a minimum risk of losing them? The answer, in theory, is simple: Study their ecology. The gardener who will not take the trouble to understand a plant's ecological needs—its complex of relationships with its environment—had better leave it where it is, and where it at least has a chance of surviving on its own. Bringing it crudely into an unwelcoming spot only helps it along the road to extinction. A plant has controlling "material resources": the texture and chemical content of the soil in which it grows, the average humidity it prefers, its exposure to sun, rain, and wind, the insects that pollinate it, the plants with which it colonizes. For example, trailing arbutus needs woody slopes, sandy, very acid soil, and the proximity of conifers, whose needles protect its roots. It prefers sunshine to shade. An attempt to establish it in a spot that only casually resembles its home ground is foredoomed to failure. Trailing abutus is particularly intolerant when moved; some other wild plants are more cooperative. Saxifrage, the "rock breaker," which actually does sometimes break rocks as it grows through them, will accommodate to most rocky, sunny spots, but sometimes will not if there is the wrong type of soil beneath the rocks. A wild plant's new home must offer some, many, or—as with the arbutus—all of the conditions it is used to, or it will die.

Interestingly, there are aberrations that cannot be explained. Trailing arbutus has been transplanted successfully, even grown from seed, not only by professionals, but by private gardeners. Presumably, they have met all its conditions. Then what of the other gardeners who have done the same—painstakingly re-created the soil, duplicated natural surroundings, nurtured it with loving care—and lost the arbutus in the second year? Is there some fractional difference in the soil, some tiny temperature variation, some magical interaction perhaps between the gardener's chemistry and the plant's? And what does one do about the exasperating wanderers—the Dutchman's-breeches and hepatica—which refuse to take root in spots hand-made to suit them, and wander away to come up in nearby places? One prays for a green thumb, and cheats by buying the next few plants from a wildflower nursery instead of digging them up in the woods.

Also, one rechecks certain key points. Drainage is particularly important to wildflowers. Clayish soil that does not absorb moisture is quick death to many of them. Ideally, every plant should be taken with a large clump of its native soil. But as this is not always possible, the wildflower gardener must equip himself with a soil-testing kit or a close rapport with his nearest agri-

159

Opposite: Wildflower garden
within formal flower
bed: Blue lobelia, black-eyed
Susan, cardinal flowers,
and prunella. Above: Fern garden
along driveway. Left: Coreopsis.
Left above: Bluebells growing
among rocks in Greece.

161

cultural station, where soil samples can be sent for testing. This is the only sure way to determine what must be done chemically to soil so that it will duplicate the acid or alkaline content and the trace minerals essential to the plants being established.

Another useful technique is to plant, whenever possible, more than one of a kind. There should always be at least two for cross-fertilization. Some plants, like the trout lilies (dogtooth violets), do best when part of a crowd—one should put down at least half a dozen of these together.

Because wildflowers are so skittish, it is sometimes easier for a gardener to concentrate on a single flower or plant so that he will have only a single set of requirements to meet. A large area devoted to one kind of plant—like the monotone or variegated heather garden—can be amazingly effective. So can a garden devoted to ferns. In the moderate zone, native ferns grow wild in the woods and forests, often beside water. For the most part they flourish in cool, shady, well-drained places, and these are minimum conditions the fern-gardener must offer if he hopes to tame them. Within the fern family there is great variety. Some, such as the Christmas fern, are evergreen. Some need acid soil; others, like the delicate maidenhair, must have neutral soil. Others are very large, like wood and ostrich ferns, or very small, like polypodies and spleenworts. The royal fern is spectacularly beautiful, but there are other ferns so nondescript they can hardly be identified. None of them should be overlooked. Each fern will add another shade of green to a fascinating monochromatic scheme and all of them exude the coolness and the sweet smell of the woods. A fern garden is best arranged as a specimen garden, with the varieties set at some distance from one another so that each shows to best advantage and has room to spread.

To the gardener who undertakes this special venture, a special warning: As the voice of the bulldozer is heard ever more the ferns are going under more quickly than all but the rarest wildflowers. It is most important that a gardener who is going to dig up wild ferns know exactly where and how to put them down for he of all people does not want to be part of the destructive forces aligned against them.

The wildflower gardener faces an almost certain destiny: Whether or not he starts out as a conservationist, he is going to finish as one. As the search continues for specimens increasingly hard to find, it will be realized how much beauty has already been destroyed by the waves of cement spreading outward from the cities—and how much more may disappear forever if not preserved in gardens. Local garden clubs and agricultural colleges are in the forefront of the crusade that hopes to block, and gradually to reverse, the trend toward a tragic destruction of the world's natural resources. In the publication *The Early American Soil Conservationist*, the United States Department of Agriculture says: "The felling of the first tree by colonists in the New World, though never mentioned by historians, was an act of great significance. It marked the beginning of an era of the most rapid rate of wasteful land use in the history of the world."

Even if wildflower gardening were not a beguiling hobby, it would be worth undertaking for a more important reason—to do whatever one could to help keep the threatened wildflowers alive.

162

Sweet-smelling,
ferny floor
of a woodland
garden.

163

9. By Still and Running Waters

"By water everything lives." More than a thousand years ago these words were set down in the holy book of the Moslems, a testament to the prescience of Mohammed. The Prophet could not have known the ramifications this statement would develop as science progressed, but he understood quite well from the evidence of his sun-baked land that where there was no water there could be no life—neither vegetable, animal, nor human.

Seventy-one per cent of the earth's surface is covered by water. This enormous mass of liquid, together with aqueous vapor in the atmosphere, constitutes the hydrosphere. Some is salt water, some fresh; all of it has fascinated man since before the Flood, and continues to become more fascinating as this century's great burst of undersea exploration reveals more about it.

There are those who love the sea so much that when they cannot be on it they are happiest living beside it, endlessly intrigued by seascapes glittering in sunlight, veiled by fog, mysterious—even menacing—under a nighttime sky. Summer visitors, fleeing overcrowded cities, rarely want or notice anything beyond the shore's clean, bared-to-the-bone beauty. Yet there are few places in the world where people live by the sea for long periods where they have not sooner or later made gardens—as if their instincts were saying, "This is a lovely place to visit, but if I'm going to live here I must have some plants growing green near me."

A seaside garden is definitely a challenge, but such gardens are some of the most beautiful in the world: in the terraced villages overhanging the Mediterranean, in the green towns that line England's seacoast, on the luxurious grounds of Newport, Rhode Island, where their stately formality reflects old Italian and French influences. Thirty miles out to sea on Nantucket Island (which is noted for its abundance of wildflowers) there are brilliant cottage gardens bursting with zinnias, hollyhocks, and hydrangeas. Further south, the peninsula of Montauk on the tip of Long Island, New York, only three miles wide, is under constant assault from strong winds carrying salt and sand, from fog, mist, driving rain, and months of scorching sun—all the typical seacoast hazards—and yet through a deliberate program of reclamation and beautification home owners there have preserved and augmented the area's vegetation. A seaside garden is largely a matter of the extra effort a gardener will put into battling the disadvantages of his site.

Nature, of course, has no trouble growing things beside and in the sea. Only to the unobservant does the scene appear to be composed only of sand, sea, and sky. In many areas—the Red Sea, for example—the water is colored by one of the numerous forms of marine algae, the primitive plants from which science has been able to deduce so much about the probable origins of life, and from which it is presently engaged in making food as well.

Other plants grow in and around the water's edge. Eel grass is familiar in tidal areas. It has heavy, rounded leaves, which are a favorite food of some wild geese and ducks. Rockweed grows on rocks in and around shallow, cool waters; the waves tear parts of it loose which in time become new plants. Irish moss grows on both sides of the Atlantic. It is rich in minerals and sulphur, and when boiled it makes a jelly

166

167

*Water
lilies bloom
like jewels
among green
leaves and
blue waters.*

that is used in some printing processes, in pharmaceutical preparations, and in beer making.

There are a number of wild plants that root happily in the thin, lean soil just beyond the sand strips. Beach plums and berry bushes — particularly huckleberry — flourish there with sea or beach grass, which sometimes travels right down onto the beach. So occasionally do shadbush, Scotch broom, chicory, evening primrose, Queen Anne's lace, and bouncing Bet. Oaks and scrub or

pitch pines make themselves quite at home in these border areas and can safely be used in a garden, as can Russian olive, locust, black pine, poplar, and London plane. Maples and tulip trees are less reliable.

The pines and Russian olive are particularly important to the seaside gardener because his first necessity is an adequate windbreak, and while substantial fences can be used, a line of these trees does an excellent job. A belt of tough sea grass to foil erosion, surrounding an inside border of sheltering

168

trees, forms a double line of defense within which knowledgeable island gardeners can proceed to grow the many plants that will accept their soil, which is usually a combination of sand with clay and rock that provides mineral matter. Protected from the wind, and periodically fed, American holly will do well; so will elderberry, pyracantha, rose of Sharon, juniper, and sedum.

A short way inland, both the plant's life, and the gardener's, are easier. The coastal rigors diminish and regular soil can be built up with humus and peat mold, supporting gardens much like those in any low-lying area. Roses especially do well near the sea; as do irises and some lilies. Beach plum can be easily domesticated, and honeysuckle will flourish. Among the flowers, perennials generally do better than annuals. Lawns are sensitive to saltwater spray, but the gardener can substitute several acceptable ground covers to bind the precious layer of topsoil and help retain its moisture: beach grass, Virginia creeper, Rosa Rugosa, bearberry, beach heather. Nor does the seaside garden have to manage without vines. Both small and large-flowered clematises are reliable in poor soil if they receive full sun, and the indomitable trumpet vine will flourish even when wind-protection is not perfect.

To inland gardeners, mulching is a seasonal chore with which they protect plants against the elements of winter; for shore gardens it is a year-round necessity. Even filtered by windbreaks, the wind will disturb the temperature and dry out the plants unless the soil around their roots is kept moist. Peat moss is particularly desirable because it holds moisture; it should be soaked when applied and kept wet (week-end gardeners will find that soaking it well on Sunday will be sufficient to keep it cool and moist all week). Salt hay is another good seaside mulch, particularly high in mineral content. There are many kinds of commercially available mulches. In some localities coffee grounds is thought of as old-wives'-tale mulching material, while in others successful gardeners swear by it. Coffee grounds can be topped with wood chips or shredded pine or coconut bark for a neater effect.

Inland water gardening (fresh-water gardening) shares the problems of the seaside garden only if the gardener's waterside spot happens to be near the shore. Anywhere else, his only concern is that he is limited to plants that are at home in or beside water. Water lilies come first to mind; if they survive transportation and adapt to the site, they will flourish without much attention. White, pink, red, rose, yellow—the colors can be mixed or concentrated, and either way the effect is lovely, with each blossom floating like an enormous jewel on its pad of leaves. They must have still or only slightly moving water, full sun, and wind protection. Open water should be left between plants to encourage new ones to come up. When divided in April or early May, they will form new colonies.

The Egyptian lotus is more delicate than our native water lily and is best grown in a hothouse or indoor pool, but an experienced gardener can risk it in a still-watered, protected pond if he removes it each autumn and allows it to rest in a dark moist sand bed over the winter. The extra trouble is many times rewarded; there are few plants as spectacular as this, and to watch its pink-tinged petals unfold is one of the great pleasures of water-gardening.

Opposite: *White
water lilies gleam in
summer sun. In distance,
pink Egyptian lotus.
Left: Close-up of lotus.
Above: Fast-growing
weeping willow shades
terrace at water's edge.*

*Artfully landscaped property
utilizes pond and paired birches
to achieve a tranquil view.*

The smaller, tougher pond lily will produce its yellow-to-orange flowers under slightly rougher conditions, including slow-streaming water, which water lilies cannot tolerate unless placed at the very edge away from any rocks (around which water will be more agitated). Both lilies grow from rhizomes rooted in the mud.

Colonies of tall pickerelweed are often found in the wild at the edge of water in which water lilies have established themselves, and a wise gardener will take this cue from nature and grow them together. The bright blue spikes are lovely beside water in naturalized effects, but also have been used with great effect against red brick around more formally styled fountains and pools.

There are other beautiful aquatic plants that will adapt to a variety of water sites. Iris lavigata prefers shallow water. Wild hyacinth and the wild forget-me-not can also be set at water's edge, as can the umbrella palm. Water snowflake is particularly charming and worth bringing in from the wild; it can be planted so that its small yellow and white blossoms float on the surface of the water. The several species of arrowhead (*Sagittaria*) are also worth seeking. In addition to their attractive arrow-shaped leaves and white blossoms, they are among the oxygenating plants which clear and freshen the water by charging it with oxygen.

Other plants to establish in shallow water are the cresses, particularly the bitter or bulbous cress (*Cardamine bulbosa*) which will be tipped with pink-tinged flowers in early spring. Jack-in-the-pulpit, trilliums, both white and brown, a variety of primula, Turk's-cap-lily, day lily, ferns—all belong at the water's edge.

Wonderful things can be planted near the water: mint, horehound, papyrus, cattail, wild rice, bulrush. Buttonbush and sweet pepper bush can be put everywhere around water, and will produce a delightful scent as they come into flower. At the inlets where the terrain is wet, but not water-logged, lovely plants will flourish which prefer very moist ground, but cannot tolerate running water. This is the place where the practiced wildflower gardener can experiment with a cardinal flower. If he buys one from a nursery the plant probably will thrive, but in the right spot and the right hands even a wild cardinal has a fair chance—and if he succeeds, the gardener will have preserved something of rare beauty.

Often the area around a small body of water lends itself particularly well to rock gardening. If a rock garden can be brought right to the water's edge the reflections of the plants will create an otherworld effect.

Most fortunate of all is the gardener who has a brook with which to work. The water itself is a delight as it bounces and bubbles along, and the brook can be made even lovelier if suitable plantings are brought to the waterside. It can become a kind of living calendar for years to come. When the brilliant golden marsh marigolds and the cresses are blooming, it is early spring. Forget-me-nots mean full summer. The spikes of the great blue lobelia signal the coming of autumn. No gardener could catch a train on the basis of this flower timetable, any more than he might with the help of Linneaus' "clock"—but, on the other hand, no calendar ever devised will cue him into each new season as beautifully as a flourishing floral "calendar" at the water's edge.

A bog offers another possibility for a water garden. It is actually a small swampy

*Right: Garden
which meets the sea.
Below: Sunken
pool is gracious
focal point
of park-like garden.*

*Left: Nantucket
roses and morning-
glories thrive
in salt air.
Below: Circular pool
reflects blooms.*

Opposite: "Park and Castle" (top) by Jan van der Heijde shows decorative use of water in 18th century. Bottom: Long Island country house with iris around pond. Left: Garden spot walled with brick has basin holding solitary pickerelweed.

place in which shallow water is held by thick layers of peat and moss. A natural bog shares with all swamps the mysterious charm of truly wild and hidden places, where one senses wildlife but does not often see it. It is a rich breeding place for plants, for centuries of the forest's growth and decay have built it into a great reserve of fertility. With care, a bog site can be created in a sheltered area, if there is a constant water supply and the foundation is properly composed of sand, peat, and humus to a depth of least a foot and a half.

Gentians will grow in a bog (though there is almost no way to be sure they will not wander as they do from any site). Cardinal flowers may do well, as may the pitcher plants which can be almost as difficult. All the more cooperative damp-loving flowers can be counted on to spring up more brilliantly and lushly from a bog than from any other site. The pickerelweeds and trout lilies and forget-me-nots will flourish along with many of the graceful grasses that are found in such sites in the wild. And it is from the bogs and swamps that the voices of the peepers come, busily announcing the arrival of spring.

All water gardens have a special charm. Walking beside a brook in any season, one understands why for the ancients such spots were haunted by water nymphs with flowing hair. And even the great seas, while they alternately serve man and threaten him, have never stopped beckoning him as well. That is why the old fierce sea gods were always partnered by glamorous females: the Mesopotamian Atargatis, the Greek Aphrodite, the Roman Venus, all symbols—as were the sirens on their deadly rocks—of water's eternal lure. The gardener who combines this elusive beauty with the fragrance and color of flowers creates a place of true enchantment.

177

10. *Plants and Life*

13.

15.

The grete herball

whiche gyueth parfyt knowlege and vnder
standyng of all maner of herbes & there gracyous vertues whiche god ha
ordeyned for our prosperous welfare and helth/for they hele & cure all man
of dyseases and sekenesses that fall or mysfortune to all maner of creatour
of god created/practysed by many expert and wyse maysters/as Auicenna
other.&c. Also it gyueth full parfyte vnderstandynge of the booke lately p
ryt by me(Peter treueris)named the noble experiens of the vertuous ha
warke of surgery.

We no longer eat roses. Rose water still is available as a cosmetic. Rose petals and violets are occasionally candied and used as confections. But "Rosée" (made of roses, nuts, sugar, spices, and capon), which appears among old recipes, and the many other floral puddings and conserves that gave variety to the diets of an earlier day, are now only curiosities. We have too rich a choice for our menus nowadays to bother with items that seem to be of marginal value. It is true that unless he goes to some trouble, the average cook does not have much opportunity to try his hand at stewed lily pods, or the numerous roots that once were eaten as the potato is now. But the chances are that he can accept the testing that time has done for him; if these foods were not bitter, mealy, tasteless, tough, or indeed possibly sickening, they would probably not have faded out of general use.

Strange things, of course—strange to those of us who live more or less in touch with the mainstream of current customs and available goods—are still eaten, particularly in hard-pressed parts of the world limited by primitive culture, difficult climate, or sheer poverty. The seeds of the yellow water lily figure largely in the vegetable diet of the Klamath Lake Indians of northern California. One species of radish (*Raphanus caudatus*, the rat-tailed radish) is grown in India not only for its root but for its edible seed pods. Western vegetable gardens grow a few greens that go by the name of mustards, but in the food-poor Far East a number of different kinds are produced with which we are not familiar. On the other end of the scale are gourmet delicacies far removed from mass consumption by high price or scarcity. Truffles are an example; so is the even more esoteric hongo, a black fungus which Mexicans who have formed a taste for it can obtain only from their cornfields after a particularly rainy season.

But for the most part, the growing things that men eat divide into fruits, vegetables, and herbs that are fairly familiar all over the "civilized" world—either because expanded agricultural knowledge makes it possible to grow them widely or because vastly speeded-up transportation facilities carry them swiftly to places where they cannot be grown. And a number of these foods can be cultivated by the gardener who is not even a farmer. Fruits, including nuts and some berries, are perhaps less easily grown. They need space and protection from pests; this makes producing them more of a nuisance than a pleasure for the average amateur. But herbs and vegetables can go hand in hand with flower gardens, particularly with cutting gardens, which, as the name implies, are grown not to create a garden but to provide cut-flower decoration for the household. Herbs, vegetables, and cutting flowers can of course be grown in separate areas, but they can be attractively—and logically—grown all together or in any practical or appealing combination. They share a function; they are grown not merely for beauty but also to be used.

They also share a certain overlapping of identification. The word "vegetable"—from the Indo-European word *weg*, meaning vigor—usually refers to plants or plant parts that are eaten. According to definition, a herb is a nonwoody plant which dies in winter down to its roots. Herbs are usually perennials or biennials and often are classed into culinary, medicinal, cosmetic, sweet-

181

smelling, or simply ornamental plants. Vegetables are usually annuals. Most cultivated as well as wildflowers are called herbaceous, because they, too, die down to the roots. The rose is included here, although it does have a woody stem and does not die to the ground in winter. However, it has no bark, which distinguishes it from other woody shrubs; it also shares with the other flower-herbs a past or present usefulness in the pharmacy and in the kitchen. The rose family is marvelously varied. Among the plants it includes are apple, strawberry, raspberry, cinquefoil, meadowsweet, and steeplebush, to name just a few.

If he wishes to, the gardener can easily make separate herb and vegetable gardens. Into the herb garden go the plants used as "extras"—for flavorings, seasonings, fragrance (as in potpourris), and soothing teas. Into the vegetable garden go the plants that come to the table as substantial parts of a meal. (And "herb," incidentally, can be pronounced with or without the h.)

The aura of romance hangs over a herb garden, the romance of legend and myth as well as that of dark and evil doings. Mustard, saffron, mint, rue, and many other herbs were as familiar in biblical times as they are to the cooks and gardeners of today.

From the sacred groves of Imhotep, the priest-physician of the second millennium who became the Egyptian god of medicine, came specifics compounded of numerous herbs still grown today. A temple papyrus dating from 1800 B.C. lists several hundred medicinal plants, including caraway, dill, a variety of mints, and myrrh. Colchicum is also listed; it is likely that the dark virtue of this member of the lily family —its poisonous root—was as highly valued

in those days of turbulent palace intrigue as were its curative properties. Aromatic herbs were burned not only to perfume the air but to drive off evil. Garlic, which in the later legends of the East sprang up in the Evil One's footsteps as he was driven out of Paradise, has been used ever since against evils both physical and spiritual. In some primitive areas it is tied around children's necks to ward off the evil eye. There are dog lovers who still swear by it as a cure for worms.

Greek and Roman medicine relied heavily on herbal remedies. Panacea, a Greek goddess of medicine, was reputed to have used them to such good effect that during the Middle Ages her name was given to the magical cure-all herb which doctors sought as diligently as alchemists sought the philosopher's stone. At various times the title was given to betony, to valerian, and to several other herbs; needless to say, none of them turned out to be the ultimate "panacea." The long list of victories claimed for betony—against weariness, wounds, drunkenness, even neurotic fear—has dwindled to its present use as a soothing tea, taken, like many other herbal teas, for headache and indigestion. Valerian (garden heliotrope) was once considered effective against epilepsy; now it is notable chiefly for its pleasant scent and its occasional use in perfume.

According to legend, the Emperor Charlemagne described herbs as "the friend of physicians and the praise of cooks." Whether he uttered the phrase is doubtful, but the seventy-four herbs that grew in his kitchen garden are a matter of record, and in those days (742-814) very little was grown or cherished that was not useful, or necessary for survival. Monastic infirmarians were

Frontispiece of *Paradisi in Sole*, with Adam, Eve, and diverse 17th-century plants.

gathering and recording all kinds of information about their herbs and other plants, information that went into fascinating and handsome herbals that have come down as literary treasures. It was chiefly from the herbals that the medieval housewife learned how to make a "salat" of mixed greens, how to combat "wind" and wounds and animal bites and even "wicked unchaste dreams." Fragrant washing-waters were made with a variety of aromatic leaves; flowers were dried and scattered in linen presses; herbs went into love potions, poisons, stimulants, sedatives, charms, messages conveyed in "the language of flowers," dyes to "make red the lips" or to color a piece of cloth—there was almost no human activity in which some garden product could not be put to good use.

Through the herbals, through "housebooks" and cookery books, and by word-of-mouth transmission of "country ways," much old herbal lore came down to succeeding generations. The New World settlers brought with them many of the old standbys, which were soon established in their dooryard gardens side by side with herbs they learned about from the Indians: bloodroot, bee balm, mallow, and many others. These gardens, as we know, were a mainstay of their lives, but by the nineteenth century, much of the medical value of herbs had been discredited. In fact, at that point, herb gardens themselves went somewhat out of fashion. The decline was temporary; in recent years, for decorative and other reasons, herb gardens have been revived.

Considering that synthetic substances have supplanted herbs in so many cases, it is surprising how many herbal preparations are still used by the pharmacist. Digitalis, the widely used heart stimulant made from foxglove, is probably the best known. But senna leaves are still brewed into tea or cooked with prunes as a laxative. A rinse made of camomile flowers is still considered a sovereign cosmetic for the hair. And from the narcotic Jimson weed, which is so old a plant that it may have provided the smoke in which the oracles of Delphi saw their visions of the future, we now derive stramonium, one of the most useful alleviants for asthma.

Woad, with whose fermented leaves the ancient Britons painted themselves blue, was once so basic to the British dye industry that a dyer was colloquially called a woader. Like most herbal dyes, it has been replaced commercially by synthetics which have much greater staying power, but a few of the old ones are still used: madder root for certain red-to-black shades and powdered alkanet root, also red, for staining pharmaceutical preparations. Alkanet's use goes far back into history. According to the Apocrypha, it was the sinful herb with which the daughters of Noah dyed their lips and cheeks in order to tempt the angels.

The modern herb garden is not called on to provide the medicaments, the soaps, the dyes, or the homemade cosmetics that came out of it in bygone days. But it is as important as ever—perhaps even more than ever—to the cook. In an era when contact between far-spread parts of the world is commonplace, travelers can return so quickly from Calcutta or Zagreb or Aix-en-Provence that they do not have time to forget the tastes of new dishes, and they often wish to duplicate them. The gourmet cook can hardly manage without certain herbs, preferably fresh and preferably from his own garden; and even the "plain" cook

184

Columbine Leaves

↓ Wild Senna

Euphorbia

↓ Rose Geranium

probably uses more than he or she realizes.

A nucleus of culinary herbs, augmented by a few fragrant herbs, can be designed into a useful and attractive herb garden. If the gardener becomes an enthusiast, this introductory list can be expanded to thirty, forty, or more herbs that are available, useful, reasonably easy to grow, and in some cases, like horehound and hyssop, almost evergreen—another asset to the winter view, which is always in need of them.

Tea rose petals can be used alone, or combined with lavender, to make a potpourri that will hold its fragrance for many months. One simple method is to dry the petals thoroughly in a cool room, away from direct sunlight, and then mix them with crushed or ground spices: cloves, cinnamon, allspice, mace. About two teaspoons of spice to six cups of petals makes a good mixture. To this should be added one to two teaspoons of powdered orris root as a fixative. After blending for five or six weeks in a large covered container, the mixture can be divided to fill several smaller containers. A few shreds of dried orange or lemon peel will intensify the mixture's pungency.

Savory, according to a herbal printed in 1525, "stirreth him that useth lechery." But it earns a place as a culinary herb because of the flavor it adds to fish, poultry, scrambled eggs, and green beans.

Larkspur, or delphinium, combines beauty and use with a vengeance. The seeds of this exceedingly attractive flower—stavesacre seeds—were used in the Middle Ages to rout head lice and are occasionally used for this purpose today.

Garden burnet leaves lend a cucumber-like taste to salads, and they can also be used to make a uniquely flavored vinegar.

186

Physician directs woman gathering medicinal herbs, 16th century. In foreground: Mandrake figures.

Far left: Delicate drawing of "Three Healing Herbs" by Albrecht Dürer. Left: Angelica, whose name evokes help of angels, was herb used to dispel plague. Above: Foxglove, which yields heart stimulant, digitalis. Right: Marvelously fragrant heliotrope.

190

Fill a clean jar half- to two-thirds full with washed and thoroughly dried leaves; pour over them heated white or cider vinegar until the jar is full. No air should remain at the top. Cover the jar tightly with a non-metallic cap and store for several weeks before using. Burnet is one of the herbs that remain green through much of the year.

Tarragon is apparently a more popular herb today than it was in the past, for there are few early references to it. A Spanish physician of the thirteenth century reported that it sweetened the breath and induced sleep. Among other culinary uses, it flavors commercially-available vinegars.

Rosemary is widely used as a flavoring, but anyone who cares to refer to *Bancke's Herbal* of 1525 may be inspired to try it for half a dozen other purposes. The flowers, scattered among clothes or books, deter the moth; a powder made of the ground flowers and worn on the person makes one "light and merry," while leaves placed under the bed drive off evil dreams. A face-wash made of the leaves boiled in white wine was recommended; and, in fact, a skin lotion made with rosemary is still sold today.

Thyme belongs to a large group of woody shrubs which serve other than culinary purposes. Thyme is used in deodorants, dentifrices, and gargles, in perfumes, and as a mask for medicinal odors. It was known in ancient Greece and still grows wild in Europe, the Himalayas, and North Africa. Thyme belongs to the mint family; most varieties are almost evergreen. One has a lemon odor; another variety is so tiny that it makes a pleasant carpet under the feet.

Lavender is probably the best known and most useful of the fragrant herbs. Even if lavender water will not preserve chastity,

as the *Hortus sanitatis* of 1491 said it would, it smells as delightful now as it did then. Spikes of it can be sewn between layers of thin fabric to make "lavender fans"; soaps, sachets, perfumes, and lotions scented with it have never lost their popularity. Curiously, medieval superstition persisted—or re-awakened—in Victorian times, when young women were advised to scent their foreheads and their handkerchiefs with it because it was thought to be an antiaphrodisiac.

Sage came as close to being a cure-all as any herb known in medieval times. It was prescribed for toothache, for palsy, for indigestion, for poisoning, for itching. In fact, according to *Bancke's Herbal*, whoever ate or drank of this herb, "it is marvel that any inconvenience should grieve them." In parts of Italy sage leaves are still eaten as an all-around health preservative, and sage tea is an enduring country remedy for headache, weak stomachs, and colds. Most cooks know it best as a seasoning for poultry, fish, pork, and cheese dishes.

Chives and shallots are members of the ancient onion family, with flavors that are more delicate than onion or garlic, but very obviously related. Chive has been grown and used for centuries in Europe and, along with onion, may have been introduced by the American colonists to the Indians. Its pretty pale violet flower gives it a double value in the herb garden.

Oregano, also called pot marjoram, is a member of the mint family. Its powerful flavor has long been familiar to Italians, but North Americans did not acquire a taste for it until fairly recently, even though it has grown wild in Mexico for generations and is used in Latin American and Mexican cooking. The seventeenth-century astrologer-

Page from late 15th-century horticultural treatise which describes ways of planting a walled-in garden.

191

physician Nicholas Culpeper was in accord with Pliny the Elder and physicians of the Middle Ages in calling it a cure for indigestion and venomous bites.

Marigold flowers once colored soups, drinks, and ointments, and was thought to be efficacious against pestilence, sprains, and failing eyesight. According to the "doctrine of signatures," a simplistic theory which claimed that plants resembled the evils they cured, marigold's strong, deep-yellow flowers made it useful against jaundice. The doctrine of signatures did not outlast the seventeenth century, but the vivid color of the marigold still makes it popular in the herb-garden border.

The neat circular herb-garden design lends itself well to a few herbs, though it might be expanded with one or two more from a group that is highly useful in cooking: dill, basil, parsley, marjoram, and perhaps even anise (a herb so valued by the colonists of Virginia that they were required to plant a few seeds of it in their new gardens, just as a Persian youth, on coming of age, was required to plant a young tree). Mint is another enormously useful herb, but it tends to run wild and force its way into every crook and cranny.

With the circular herb garden on page 200, there is a companion plan for a vegetable garden-in-the-round, an arrangement that makes a decorative asset out of plantings that are usually put in utilitarian straight rows and concealed as much as possible from the public eye. Unless one is an expert, vegetable gardening is a particular kind of madness. Most amateurs agree that it costs them more to grow their own produce than it would to buy it even at the most superior markets; that the culture and care can be back-breaking; that rabbits and woodchucks and crows often reap the harvest before the owner has had a chance to find out if the lettuce is coming up bitter. Yet there is a special excitement in growing even a small portion of one's own food. A richly red, firm tomato plucked from a plant growing just beyond the kitchen door, served on a bed of crisp romaine whose progress also has been under observation since its first sparse shoots speared up through the ground, is somehow nothing at all like the tomato one carries home from the market. This is not an illusion; it probably has more taste, more vitamin content, and has been exposed to fewer chemical adulterants than commercially grown vegetables. What matter if it costs at least half-again as much, on the average, than store-bought produce?

The vegetables in the circular plan combine fairly neat growth habit with general popularity for the Anglo-American table. But this does not mean that they are all English or American natives. Having learned how many flowering plants, so widely grown here that we claim them as indigenous, actually originated in far parts of the world, it comes as no surprise that the vegetables which are more basic to man's existence have traveled with him even longer and farther.

Roughly seven thousand years ago, when Neolithic man graduated from the pointed stick to the simple hoe and settled down to an agricultural existence, his first vegetables appear to have been wild grasses, wheat, and barley. Green plants came under cultivation soon afterward; the Lord reminds Noah that "as I gave you the green plants, I give you everything," and elsewhere in the Bible many fruits, herbs, and vegetables are named.

Lettuce may have been among the "bitter herbs" mentioned in the Bible. The Romans, it is said, found a way of preserving salad out of season by a mixture of honey and vinegar. In our gardens we grow tight, crisp lettuce, of which Bibb lettuce is the most palatable; "leaf" lettuce, with many more outer leaves than the crisp type; and the cylindrical Cos or Romaine varieties.

Cabbage, which probably originated in Asia, was once thought to have been introduced throughout Europe by the Romans, but the testimony of language hints that it may actually have come, along with many other cultural, governmental, and religious innovations, with the raiding Celts, who from about 1000 B.C. to the beginning of the Christian era were spreading their influence from the Mediterranean to Denmark and Britain.

The evidence of language supplies some of the botanical investigator's chief clues as he strives to pinpoint, in time and place, the origins of plants. Particularly as they concern food plants, these researches are immensely important not only to archeologists and anthropologists but in a practical sense to agriculturists, because a primitive form of a food plant can guide breeders in their continuing efforts to improve crops. It is a fascinating and frustrating form of scientific detection. By the time man started to keep written records, he had been a wanderer for generations, carrying plant materials, among other things, over so much of the world that many of them may never be traced to their sources. Even without writing, there are clues to antiquity when ancient and datable artifacts depict a plant, as the Cretan murals show roses and the Egyptian ones show palm fronds and lotus, but these cannot establish where the plant came from in the first place. Inferences must be pieced together from fairly fragile evidence; for example, the existence of many names for a given plant in a primitive country, where

Beautifully conceived herb garden in manner of 18th-century England. Brick walk divides planted beds.

193

There is beauty—often
overlooked—in the forms and colors
of vegetable plants, such as
leek (top left), purple cauliflower
(top right), and zucchini (left).
Cabbage (above) is blessed
with one of the most luscious
greens in all nature.

195

communication between settlements is necessarily poor, suggests that the plant grows spontaneously throughout the area and so may have originated there, but this is hardly proof. The existence of many wild forms of a plant in a given area is also taken as an indication that it is native to the area and may have had its genesis there. In the future, much significant data may come from the increasingly sophisticated study of chromosomes, which has already established relationships between plants in such widely separated parts of the world that neither historians nor geologists can as yet conclusively explain their distribution.

By these and other means, we know that the tomato, which circles the birdbath in our vegetable plan, has had a peripatetic history. From the number of wild forms that exist in the Andean regions of South America, it appears to have originated there and to have traveled up through Central America and Mexico, along with maize, in some ancient migration. Maize, of course, continued northward to become a staple of the North American Indian and eventually of the colonists, but the tomato did not advance above Mexico until the sixteenth century. Even then, it was imported into Italy and to other parts of Europe before North Americans finally became interested in growing and eating it. Thomas Jefferson, in 1781, was probably one of the first Americans to experiment with it. The French found it attractive enough to call it *pomme d'amour*, which translated into the early English nickname "love apple."

The string bean—also called the snap bean, as most modern varieties are stringless—is an American native. Although it may have originated in South or Central America,

it was being intensively cultivated by the northern Indians when the white man arrived. Several kinds of beans, including lima beans, were important in the Indian diet when meat was hard to come by. While they could not have known that beans are comparatively high in protein, they knew from practical experience that a mixture of beans and maize (the bean-and-corn dish which we still call by the Indian name succotash) was filling and strengthening, and from them the colonists learned to sustain themselves through the long and difficult winters of New England with this combination of protein and carbohydrate.

The history of the cucumber is somewhat obscure. Our name for it comes from the Latin *cucumis*, but the presence in India of several plant species related to the cucumber indicates that it may have originated somewhere between the Himalayas and the Bay of Bengal. It can be traced westward by the many names that exist for it in languages along the way, in Aryan, Greek, Arabic, and Armenian. There is some evidence that it was grown in China in the second century B.C. It grew in Charlemagne's garden in the ninth century, and came to the New World with Columbus in the fifteenth. There is a wild cucumber, also called balsam-apple, which grows in our thickets and waste places; gourds, melons, and pumpkins also belong to this large family. Cucumber is still considered to have virtue as a cosmetic. At one time, the French grew a particular variety of it for this purpose, and today the ordinary cucumber is still used, sliced or liquified, as a stimulant and astringent for the skin.

Like the American Indian, the garden pepper received its name because of Colum-

196

bus's mistaken belief that the islands he reached in 1492 were indeed part of the India he had set out to reach. The capsicum which the natives grew and ate were pungent, and he believed them to be related to the Far Eastern pepper plants—an important item in the spice trade which had to a great extent motivated his voyage. The true pepper plant, *Piper nigrum*, is an entirely different plant; if Columbus had encountered the sweet, smooth variety of green pepper now popular in North America, he would have appreciated the difference.

Broccoli, like cauliflower, is related to the cabbage; it is a cultigen, i.e., a plant originated in cultivation. Pliny reports it in the first century, and it was always valued by the Italians, but a taste for its strong flavor apparently had to be acquired by the Anglo-Saxons. Although it has been grown in America for about two hundred years, it became an important vegetable only thirty or forty years ago when the interesting foods of Italian-Americans began to influence the diets of their neighbors.

Eggplant probably originated in India, where many names for it are found in Sanskrit and in Bengali, and in the Hindustani languages. A small-fruited kind was known in ancient China; the eggplant we know reached the West only about fifteen hundred years ago. There are no Greek or Roman names for eggplant, and this plus the fact that it does appear in Arabic and in North African languages leads to the deduction that it was one of the plants brought into the Mediterranean region during the Arab invasions of the Middle Ages. Eggplant can be grown in yellow, red, white, greenish and even striped forms, in addition to the rich purple which is most familiar.

Botanical drawings of varieties of peas. Culinary and medicinal plants were planted with flowering herbs.

197

Many plants with edible roots are believed to have originated around the Mediterranean. The wild carrot is well known to us as Queen Anne's lace; early in time its roots developed into the vegetable we know today. Greek physicians promoted it as a curative plant; while there is little evidence for it as a specific for stomach ailments or poor eyesight, modern nutritionists concur that it is rich in vitamin A and that indeed it is a desirable food.

To those familiar only with the fleshy red root of the beet, it comes as a surprise that it belongs to the same family as the leafy, spinach-like Swiss chard. Tender young beet greens can also be eaten, either as a potherb or raw in salads, and in fact seem to have been used as a vegetable before the root was considered good for anything other than medicinal purposes. The Romans experimented with it in the second and third centuries, but there is no record that it was cultivated for food until the fourteenth century in England. The beet is still a slowly acquired taste for many, but it is easy to grow. At the very least, the red-veined leaves are decorative in the vegetable garden.

The zinnias that edge the circular vegetable garden claim no place as either herb or vegetable, but they provide wonderful and reliable cut flowers for the house. Marigolds might be substituted, or snapdragons, or any other annuals that are not too tall; or, the border might be deepened to include two rows of different flowers. From the gardener's viewpoint, everything in the circular plan is expendable—or at least grown to be used; but if it is well planned and cared for, the garden-in-the-round will remain pleasing to the eye even as it is being thinned for the benefit of the table.

198

Herb Garden

Inner Circle: 1. Birdbath, Hybrid Tea Roses
Second Circle: 2. Summer Savory, 3. Delphiniums, 4. Garden Burnet, 5. Tarragon
Third Circle: 6. Rosemary, 7. Variegated Thyme, 8. Silver Thyme, 9. Lavender
Fourth Circle: 10. Dwarf Sage, 11. Chives, 12. Oregano, 13. Shallots
Outer Circle: 14. Pot Marigolds

Vegetable Garden

Inner Circle: 1. Sundial, Tomatoes
Second Circle: 2 and 4, String Beans; 3 and 5, Cucumbers
Third Circle: 6. Green Peppers, 7. Broccoli, 8. Eggplant, 9. Cabbage
Fourth Circle: 10. Buttercrunch Lettuce, 11. Carrots, 12. Beets, 13. Romaine
Outer Circle: 14. Lilliput Zinnias

11. *Cities in Flower*

"We need the tonic of wildness," Henry David Thoreau wrote in *Walden* in 1854. "We must be refreshed by the sight of inexhaustible vigor, vast and Titanic features, the seacoast with its wrecks, the wilderness with its living and decaying trees...we need to witness our own limits transgressed."

It is a long way from Thoreau's "Titanic features" to today's city parks—particularly to such desperate half-measures as the small vest-pocket parks which have begun to appear between the skyscrapers in our crowded cities. Some of these, like Paley Park in New York which includes a waterfall, the sound of which actually dims the noise of traffic, are beautifully landscaped; some are scarcely more than strips of cement just large enough to hold a few benches and trees in tubs. Probably the wildest aspect of nature to be seen there would be the struggle of an ant with a large crumb or a confrontation between a bird and an earthworm. Yet these tiny areas, like all parks, are token acknowledgement of the need Thoreau recognized—the need of human beings, particularly urban residents, to be able to sit occasionally and contemplate something other than man-made, mechanized turmoil.

From the time men first began to congregate in cities they have been aware of this need, even when they had no way of expressing it nor any chance of satisfying it. The Assyrian kings who on special occasions allowed the public into their vast private parks must have known that this brief exposure to space and beauty would help to convince their subjects that they were living under the best of rulers. The Persians, to whom trees were so important that a man who planted and cared for them had a better chance of getting into the Zoroastrian heaven than one who did not, provided parks especially for the public—though, shortsightedly, these parks were most often set outside the urban areas, inaccessible to those who needed them most.

Citizens of the Greek city-states were more fortunate. They had access to landscaped areas around the principal buildings and to public entertainment grounds, as well as to the sacred groves surrounding the temples. When Rome became so crowded that the wealthy began to move out of the city, the emperors began to create public parks where they could to divert the poor from their increasingly intolerable lot.

But in the closed societies of the early Middle Ages, when the poor were barely conceded the right to exist, parks were fabled, jealously guarded areas behind castle and monastery walls—part of the privilege which the church, the nobility, and, eventually, the rich merchants reserved for themselves. Down through the eighteenth century the game-stocked preserves of the landed English were rigidly protected from mere trespass, while to trap a rabbit or shoot a deer on the overlord's land, the crime of poaching, was punishable by death. However, around most villages, there was grazing land to which the villagers held common rights. The commons, which gradually developed into community meeting places and greens for bowling and cricket, were recreated in the villages of New England. What was probably the first public park in the United States grew out of Boston Common, which was set aside in 1634 as communal pasture land for sheep, in the tradition of the mother country.

204

Above: City garden has flagged patio for outdoor entertaining.
Right: Municipal garden, New Castle, Pennsylvania.
Opposite: Small city garden manages nicely alongside garage.

206

Despite the commons, which evolved almost accidentally into recreational areas, there was no real concept of sizable, landscaped public parks in Europe until the revolutionary turmoil of the eighteenth century forced the powerful to realize that many of their prerogatives could no longer be denied the people. London's Hyde Park was an exception. Originally, its more than fifteen hundred acres were the manor of Hyde, in the holding of Westminster Abbey. Henry VIII preempted it as a royal preserve when he dissolved the monasteries, but in the seventeenth century James I opened it to the public and it became one of the favorite pleasure grounds of Stuart England. Other great English parks, however, like the elegant St. James, were to some extent reserved for the upper classes—sometimes by the expedient of an admission charge—and came only gradually into free public use. Not until after the French Revolution were the great royal gardens of Europe truly open to everyone. Versailles and Le Petit Trianon, near Paris, the magnificent botanical and zoological gardens of Schönbrunn and the Belvedere in Vienna—these are among the stately parks which were conceived for private pleasure but now are open to all.

These spectacular old parks are an inheritance from the past. Like broad, tree-lined avenues built in great cities for royal and military display, they are frequently located in the central or elegant sections where they have no relevance to the daily life of the poor. Yet the question of who should enjoy the land, and how, could no longer be ignored. From the middle of the nineteenth century, far-sighted city planners and sociologists, perceiving the increasingly stifling and dehumanizing conditions of city life, tried to plan and implement more prudent land use. In America the frontier had already been pushed to its western limits, but between the two oceans some of the vast and beautiful wilderness remained. It was evident that unless deliberate steps were taken to keep it free every acre of it eventually would be despoiled.

To protect this heritage, Congress in 1891 empowered the president to set aside national forest preserves, beginning with hundreds of thousands of acres in Wyoming. In 1907 these lands were designated National Forests and now comprise fourteen million acres of open spaces, nature and game preserves, and majestic vistas, chiefly in the West.

Washington, D.C.,
plantings. Above: Plan
for Lafayette
Park, facing White House.
Top right: Completed
planting (ground view).
Islands of quiet:
Mellon Park (middle) and
Emmet Park (bottom).

Parks and forests, however, do not benefit those who cannot get to them. The situation was already serious when the nineteenth-century planners worked to create parks in cities that were even then mushrooming, and it is even more difficult today. As the cities swelled, swallowing up the marginal green areas that had once surrounded them, their residents needed the relief of leaves and flowers and fresh air more than ever. Yet the more crowded the cities became, the more land was worth. And, regrettably, it was much more profitable to put up a new building than to clear space for parks. Many park projects were dissolved in the crossfire between real estate and political interests. Chicago, St. Louis, and Pittsburgh are among the cities that attempted, while still in a formative state, to set aside land for beautification and recreation, only to have it lost

by the relentless surge of private interest.

Nevertheless, the park systems that were established during the second half of the nineteenth century have helped to keep our major cities from choking to death, though sometimes aesthetics and better living were not the first considerations of the city fathers. Central Park, one of New York City's greatest assets, was a political football for years before designers Frederick Law Olmsted and Calvert Vaux finally were allowed to create it from the shambles of grazing land and the shantytown that disfigured the city's northern extreme. In fact, it remained a political convenience for some time. Hundreds of men who became unemployed in the financial panic of 1857 worked in its construction and landscaping. Central Park was the prototype for many parks that Olmsted went on to design: Pros-

*Opposite:
View of
18th-century
Vienna
by Canaletto
emphasizes long
open walks
beside formal
gardens.
Left: Flowery
island runs
length of New
York's Park
Avenue.*

211

Opposite:
Elegant Paley
Park in
midtown
Manhattan.
Left: Roman
public garden,
17th century.
Below: New York's
Ford Foundation
building
encloses garden
with glass
curtain-walls.

pect Park in Brooklyn, South Park in Chicago, Mt. Royal Park in Montreal, and the parks of Buffalo and Boston.

From time to time many American cities have self-styled themselves "garden cities." It is possible that Washington one day may really deserve the description. Like all large cities, it has its slums; but currently intensive efforts are being made to realize the precept of the city's original architect, Pierre L'Enfant, that "parks and open spaces are not an afterthought but the prerequisite for structuring the growth of the community along lines equally sound and beautiful."

Washington now has eight hundred parks. The wild areas of Rock Creek and the experimental water design and construction of Meridian Hill are among its great ornaments, and, in 1940, Mr. and Mrs. Robert Woods Bliss gave part of their spectacular Dumbarton Oaks estate to the nation to be used as a state park. Washington cannot hide its typical urban problems, but each year parts of it become more beautiful.

For the individual, the problems of creating a city garden are not really so different from the ones you encounter in making a country garden. The components are the same, but their dimensions necessarily are smaller and usually there are urban problems it may take some ingenuity to overcome.

If partial or filtered sun is available, a number of spring- and summer-blooming wildflowers will flourish in as little as a foot of soil; among them: bee balm, bergamot, black-eyed Susan, bouncing Bet, and bloodroot. Some of the tougher ferns—Christmas fern, for example—will grow in shade. Privet does well; so does pyracantha. Evergreens are difficult except for yew and hemlock. House plants will do well in a city garden if they are cleaned and sprayed often.

Kitchen gardens are possible. Design them carefully, like a medieval monastery garden. The texture and color of many herbal leaves can do much to enhance a south wall, and since many herbs are annuals new excitement can be created each year.

The planting of penthouse terraces today is a privilege of the very rich, but there are other kinds of roof gardens that can be developed with simple materials and a little imagination. The flat, asphalt roof of an apartment house will support wooden-slat flooring, a fence, and flower tubs, which can provide restful places of a hot evening if they are effectively grouped.

Beyond this, there are few ways in which an individual can make a city bloom. By and large the improvement must come from concerted, official action, as it has done in the genuine garden city of Columbia, Maryland. Intimacy with nature has been provided as one of the city's vital functions. In the downtown area, citizens pursue their activities near forty acres of parkland, including a grove of two-hundred-year-old oaks. Lakes and garden space and provisions for every kind of outdoor recreation have been built into the design with such care and flexibility that it seems improbable that they will be outgrown in the foreseeable future.

One thing is certain. Man will find it increasingly difficult to live in cities unless they are improved. Parks help, but neither they nor the dusty plant on the windowsill can bring enough natural beauty into the city resident's life to revitalize it. The new garden cities may be one answer. Another may lie in drastic rebuilding; such plans are only suggestions at the present, but one day they may be translated into reality.

Top: Mid-17th century "embroidered" French garden, with trellised background. Bottom: Columbia, planned city between Washington, D.C., and Baltimore.

12. *World Within*

The dedicated gardener can be identified by the fact that he cannot live a long winter indoors without some verdant life near him to admire and to tend. His indoor garden may be one pot on a kitchen windowsill or an elaborate display of large, exotic potted plants; in either case it represents the whole green world from which he has temporarily been cut off by winter. Luckily, for these "men of flowers"— and for the urbanites and the house-bound whose gardens must always be confined to the indoors—"window gardening" is a term not to be taken literally. A garden can spring from a specially built container, a table top, or a sunken section of floor, or it can cling to a rough wall. Formulated plant foods and soils, the ability to control temperature and humidity, and books full of expert advice now make it possible for the novice who begins with a dime-store philodendron eventually to find every room in his house, including the bathroom, supporting lush greenery.

He will not achieve this glory, however, without meeting conditions which the outdoor gardener can be more lax in observing. He must be disciplined, vigilant, and so attached to his plants that caring for them is a pleasure. Like pets, house plants need daily care, and if the care is not inspired by a kind of affection it becomes nothing but a round of irksome chores.

Growing plants indoors is no more a new activity than is any other kind of gardening. The potted plants that decorated the terraces of the ancient East surely were brought indoors from time to time. In cold regions where all food is precious, cooks have tried for hundreds of years to keep herbs and vegetables alive and growing over the winter. About the middle of the eighteenth century, when faster ships and expanding trade put Europe in closer touch with parts of the world that had previously been remote, indoor gardens shared in the new plant riches that began to arrive from the Americas, Africa, and the East. Orangeries and conservatories bloomed with dozens of new varieties. While today relatively few homes run to such luxuries (though the prefabricated greenhouse is increasingly available and practical) the hobby of indoor gardening has never fallen from favor.

There have been fashions in plants—the potted palm, the aspidistra, the rubber plant —all have been in and out of vogue. For years the umbrella stand shared the entrance hall with a Boston fern in a pedestaled planter, and the "snake plant"— a sansevieria —stood stiffly on the windowsill between the geranium and the ivy. As new varieties of philodendron with larger, more exotically shaped leaves arrived from the jungles of Central and South America, the philodendron graduated from the window box and the hanging pot to containers so large they could be considered furniture. The popularity of the African violet has spread far and wide recently, and logically, for the size of these lush plants is suited to the smallest apartment and they will flower all winter even in poor light as long as their few fundamental needs are supplied.

Keeping plants indoors, then, is not new. What is new is the growing tendency to arrange these plants not as a conservatory collection or in a neat windowsill row, but as a true garden, planned as carefully for good proportion, interesting contrast, and attractive color as the outdoor garden. Con-

Preceding pages: East Indian influence suffuses floral print of 18th-century English cotton. Inset: Indoor garden in a south window. Opposite: "Flowers in Blue Vase," by Mary Scott, painted 1828.

218

Artificial light of "grow lamps" does as well as sunshine in nurturing primrose seedlings (right) and mature plants (below).

temporary architecture and furniture have had a great deal to do with this development. Disturbed by the embellished rooms of earlier decades, we now welcome open rooms that flow into one another, and simple, clean-lined furniture that seems to offer relief from what more and more people have come to consider a cluttered way of life. The eye can weary of simplicity, too; and those who occupy the open spaces find that they often need to be divided and blocked off for the practicalities of living. Large, floor-based plants—even small trees in tubs—are one way to achieve this minimal demarcation. Further, plants — even more than paintings or objets d'art — provide a vitality and patterning that make these sometimes sterile backgrounds come alive.

A well-planned indoor garden that suits its setting is as much at home with new contemporary styles as it was with the old, as it can be even with antiques.

Indoor gardens can be created in many different ways. Windowsills and windowsill extensions are the most obvious, but even a beginner need not stop at these. Glass shelves can be placed across a window, particularly one with an unattractive view, to hold small plants. Vines such as philodendron can be trained around a window frame. Tea wagons and tier tables can be used as mobile gardens, moved as desired, so long as the plants are not exposed to drafts or extreme changes of temperature. Plenty of expert help is available for the gardener who wants to build a terrarium or a dish garden, miniature delights most welcome where space is limited.

For drama in a properly lit setting, the most effective "garden" might be simply a single outstanding plant. This is especially true for the begonia or orchid fancier who disdains a mass display, preferring to show his treasures in individual splendor as jewelers show important gems.

Many architects now design indoor gardens as an intrinsic part of buildings. In a private home, this probably is a metal-lined section sunk into a room divider, a bookcase, or, most effectively, a section of floor beneath a window—a device that can be adapted successfully to older houses as well!. In such an area, even a little care and taste are almost guaranteed to produce a dramatic effect. One or two tall, bold plants—palms, large-leaved caladiums, rubber plants—can be combined with something of softer foliage and perhaps a small piece of sculpture to create an effect of oneness between the room and the out-of-doors. These green, living areas may recall the courtyards of Spain and the peristyles of Greece and Rome.

Bringing a plant indoors does not change its basic needs and habits, and the greatest help a gardener can have is reliable information concerning its original environment. Many house plants are tropical or semitropical in origin, yet they are widely divergent in habit, particularly in relation to light, reacting just as they would outdoors to changes in day length and light intensity. Some, like poinsettias, flower only when the day is short, while others respond better to longer periods of light and more, rather than less, warmth. For many of them, growth slows or stops during the bleak winter days just as it would outdoors, and they even may appear to be moribund. One of the joys of an indoor garden is that as early as January plants respond to seasonal changes, long before we are aware of them. Then the garden repays the care that has been lavished

221

on it by producing shoots and buds while February winds are still whipping naked branches on the other side of the window.

In this accelerated activity, light is crucial. Greenhouses produce their year-round miracles of growth and bloom by providing optimum conditions of every kind—not the least of which is that their glass walls and angled roofs take advantage of every bit of available light. But recent experiments have taught us that similar miracles can be produced in the most modest indoor garden through the use of artificial light.

A few plants may be stimulated slightly by lamplight, though care must be taken not to expose them too closely or for too long a time to avoid burning the leaves. However, astonishing results have been achieved with special fluorescent lighting— the basis for a new subdivision of horticulture called light gardening.

A light garden may be as elaborate, decorative, and costly as the gardener cares to make it, or it may be assembled with articles from the corner hardware store. Simple or elaborate, however, it is not a hobby for the untutored beginner. Not every fluorescent lamp will help create green and flowering miracles. Many of the so-called "daylight" lamps on the market will have no effect at all on plants. The best results have been achieved with lamps, specially designed for light gardening, which produce a pinkish fluorescent light high in the blue-red rays which are most beneficial to plants—the rays to which they respond in natural light. An-

222

other advantage of growing plants in this manner is that it can be done in basements and out-of-the-way service rooms.

Working with these lamps is exciting, well worth the risk of a few initial disappointments that may result from inexperience. The sustained, even light must be balanced by adjustments in temperature and humidity which the gardener can only learn to make, in his particular environment, by experiment. Experiment must also determine how far above the plants the lamps should be placed (adjustable shelves are best for this purpose) and the proper settings for the automatic timer that turns the light on and off at predetermined intervals.

All of this is quite different from putting a pot of geraniums on the windowsill and watering them now and then. The gardener may feel that so much gadgetry separates him from his original aim, which was to have something lovely to look at and to get his hands, if only in a small way, into the soil. But he will see results that his hands, however "green," could not have performed. Seeds will begin to sprout after only a few days. The action is so fast that it might be likened to time-lapse photography. Tiny leaves appear; the stems grow tall; buds form and open, and then one day a flower is complete.

Under this surrogate sunlight, vegetables and herbs can be forced with great success. Many flowering plants including primroses, impatiens, fuchsia, begonias, and gloxinias can be brought from seed to full bloom in two or three months, even less, depending on—though always accelerating—the plant's intrinsic growth pattern.

Humidity is the second factor which the indoor gardener, standing in for nature, must control. If the air is too dry, transpiration is speeded up and the plant becomes dehydrated. The first sign of flaccidity in leaves or stems signals an emergency, which should be treated at once to prevent permanent damage to the roots.

It can be assumed that the air in most homes is too dry for most plants, and that they will prosper better if the humidity is raised by some automatic device. An electrically controlled humidifier will accomplish this, but a simpler arrangement is to set

224

Opposite: Most nurseries have shade house to protect young plants. Above left: Browallia, tropical American herb, gets start in greenhouse. Left: South windows are excellent hothouses. Above right: Inside plant gallery is year-long pleasure.

225

Left: Orchid greenhouse is addition to kitchen. Below: Orchids growing in baskets. Right: Outside view of greenhouse, with bird feeders.

the indoor garden in a waterproof tray containing a shallow bed of pebbles, gravel, sand, moss, or any material that can be kept damp by one or two waterings a day. The tray should not be drenched; the object is not to water the plants from below, but to provide only enough moisture for evaporation around the plants, supplying the humidity they need. The only plants that will not benefit from this are the succulents, like desert cacti, which have adapted to their arid environment by storing water in their leaves and stems and which may be harmed

by an oversupply. Spraying will also help. It should be one of the daily routines, in any case, for it dusts the leaves, grooming them to their shiny best, and discourages fungi and insect pests. It should also be remembered that a single plant does not fare as well as a group of plants, which help to humidify their environment by their own transpiration.

Temperature is perhaps the easiest factor to regulate. In nature, plants must adjust in every climate to variable temperatures during the day and a drop at night, and

226

therefore when a healthy plant is brought indoors it will be tolerant of moderate highs and lows. A range of sixty-five to seventy-five degrees Fahrenheit during the day to fifty degrees at night will be acceptable to most plants, and is necessary for some; fuchsias and camellias, for example, will not flower well without cool nights. It is in the dark, cool hours that the food created during the day by photosynthesis is transformed chemically into usable carbohydrates and distributed throughout the plant's structure. These general rules do not apply to all house plants. Requirements of individual plants should always be checked, and plants should be grouped with others from the same environment which can be expected to flourish under similar conditions. And, of course, no plant should be placed in a draft. Excluding the light garden, a south window is the best place to grow most kinds of house plants.

If, when thinking of house plants, geraniums come first to mind, it is with good reason: Geraniums are among the easiest indoor plants to grow. They bloom reliably

227

A

B

C

D

*Exotic plants which
grow well indoors:
A) kalanchoe,
South African succulent
with tiny red buds;
B) Christmas-cactus
(flower); C) cyclamen
(close-up); D) primrose;
E) heliocereus,
cactus from Mexico.* E

year after year, and usually more than once a year. Cuttings are rooted easily in water and a whole geranium garden can eventually be born of one healthy plant. There are gardeners with a special touch who have succeeded in growing so-called "geranium trees" four feet high. If this is attempted it should be remembered that these plants like their roots crowded and should not be overwatered, and that while all three colors—white, pink, and red—are reliable and durable, the reds seem to be especially tough.

African violets are indoor plants all year, and they should be grown in or near a north window. There are also amaryllis, a remarkable plant that can be kept dormant for as long as one wishes and needs only to be brought into the light to start blooming again; lantana, which blooms all year whether inside or out; cyclamen, which is unpredictable, blooming magnificently for some gardeners but not as easily for others, an unexplained gardening mystery. Gloxinias, begonia, fuchsia, chrysanthemums, primulae—all of these can be grown indoors, and generally in a southern exposure. Primulae, however, grow most spectacularly under the pink fluorescent lamps.

The indoor gardener must be prepared to experiment. If a plant does not do well where the book says it should, move it. A southern window may have a bit too much sun for a begonia, a bit too little for a chrysanthemum. Neither the book nor the florist can have all the right answers for a specific situation; a successful indoor gardener must find them himself.

Flowering shrubs sound ambitious, but can be cultivated indoors with wonderful results—especially gardenias, camellias, and azaleas. Perhaps because of the inevitable urban smog and soot, gardenias are a little more reliable in the country than in town; but enormous gardenia shrubs have been kept in beautiful flower in city apartments, and the work they require is rewarded a hundredfold by the shiny white flowers and the intoxicating scent. Camellias are somewhat more cooperative and, although without scent, the flowers, in many variations of color from white to deep red, are most decorative.

The desert cacti are popular indoor plants and easily grown. For the most part they are interesting rather than beautiful, but the Christmas and Thanksgiving cacti produce spectacular blossoms. The Christmas cactus, which appropriately blooms around Christmas, produces pink flowers at the ends of what appear to be leaves but actually are branches. If it likes its location, it may send out a few more flowers in the spring. The Thanksgiving cactus has slightly different leaves and a salmon-pink flower; it, too, may bloom at odd times. Another desert succulent is the echeveria, one of the most successful plants for a sunny windowsill and one of the easiest to propagate. A leaf from the main stem laid upon the soil will take root and produce a new plant with lovely pink blossoms. Incidentally, it is not true that succulents need direct sunshine the entire day.

There are many nonblooming foliage plants that will fill an indoor garden with a variety of leaf shapes and color, and some of these are especially important where no southern exposure is available. Ferns, for example, adapted to survival on damp forest floors, dry out quickly in a southern light, and prefer any other exposure as long as

Opposite: Hothouse window frame attached to living room.
Left: View from inside.
Below: Arrangement of fall leaves, berries, and stones is another form of indoor gardening.

the humidity is high and they are protected from extreme cold. There are also house plants which grow in semidarkness, making it possible to place them almost anywhere. Some people have been successful, for instance, in keeping polypody fern, which they brought in from the woods, year after year on their living-room coffee table.

As with all house plants, it is safest to buy cultivated ferns from a nursery. Wild ones, even those brought in from one's own garden, are not likely to survive. Enough cultivated ferns are available to furnish a whole indoor garden with varied foliage ranging from the feathery Boston to the broad and more unusual bird's-nest and rabbit-foot ferns.

Indoor gardening is full of small-scale pleasures. Tending plants daily, it is astonishing to find that they vary so much that they almost seem to develop personalities. The intimate contact brings rewards not always available from outdoor gardens — watching a plant respond as one learns its particular needs; waiting attentively for a single new bud to flower; learning, not in a generalized way, but from the evidence right in the palm of one's hand that each leaf truly is a little different from every other leaf on the same plant.

231

13. *A Place for Meditation*

"By its very nature a garden is an area removed from the daily intrusions of the outside world. Even in our big cities there are odd and unexpected places—often not even green—dedicated to shutting out whatever disturbs the senses. They offer a chance to halt for a few moments of spiritual repair before slipping back into the blasting, buffeting fray of everyday living. Many of London's squares are used in this manner. People go out of their way to walk through them, and when there are no benches they lean against the railings and stare at the pigeons. People gravitate by instinct to any spot where water is combined with even the dustiest greenery; around the Plaza fountain in Manhattan or in London's Trafalgar Square there are always dozens of spectators watching the water as if mesmerized. In downtown New York, on one of the busiest corners in the world, the anachronism of little Trinity Church stands pat and prim in its seventeenth-century churchyard, protected only by a scraggly hedge, an iron paling, and its own indomitable calm from the turbulence around it. And as Wall Street workers stream out of their frenetic offices at noon, some of them drift into Trinity's pocket-sized cemetery, to turn the sooty grass and time-tilted gravestones into a peaceful midday retreat. The hunger and the need are obvious. Human beings have always needed to be able to sit alone at times and think; and at our tempestuous point in history, we need this more than ever.

But there is a special sense in which the word meditation is used by artists, by philosophers, by the troubled in search of tranquility—a sense in which meditation becomes an effort not to retreat but to perform a positive act of internal re-creation. It is in this sense that the men of the Bible, like Isaac, "went forth to meditate"—it is meditation as the reverent and sustained contemplation of a theme, a thought, a feeling, an ideal. And we seem to do it best when we are surrounded by trees, plants, and flowers.

The growing things of the earth have always been associated with man's most deeply felt moments: with victory, love, birth, death. A recently excavated cave in the Zagros Mountains of Iraq yielded up the burial place of a Neanderthal man laid to rest some 60,000 years ago on a bed of boughs which a companion—someone we barely acknowledge as human in our terms —had taken the trouble to interweave with flowers. We have seen that flowers and plants accompanied worship in almost all known religions; they were endowed with special significance from the perorations in the Egyptian Book of the Dead down through the centuries to the floral symbolism of the Gothic ages. Even today they appear at ceremonies, not only as decoration but as a survival of ancient meanings and customs in man's long relationship with his gods, and as a reminder that in their presence he has always been able to approach more closely to a state of oneness between himself and his world. And there are certain kinds of gardens, even certain spots in gardens, which have a particular power to stimulate man's capacity to communicate in this way with his innermost self.

Chinese gardens, both before and after Buddhism largely supplanted Taoism in the first century A.D., were often consciously designed for this kind of meditation. Time and war have destroyed these ancient

Preceding pages: Bishop's Gardens of Washington (D.C.) Cathedral. Opposite: Woodcut of monk in 15th-century monastery garden.

234

236

Opposite: Zen garden of Hammond Museum, North Salem, New York. Left: Small stone Bodhisattva on island of Hammond Lake.

gardens. We can learn about them now only from porcelains, paintings, and ancient documents. Some of their picturesque aspects were copied in the English "Chinese" gardens that sprang up in the eighteenth century, the pagoda at Kew, for instance, or an occasional "moon-gate," the original meaning of which has disappeared into the mists of time. Each rock and tree and flower in these gardens possessed a significance complicated also by their relationships to one another. These meanings are almost as much of a mystery to us as they were to Marco Polo, who first reported, in the thirteenth century, the splendors of China's "many exotic gardens."

Everything in a Chinese garden was symbolic and designed to lead the mind beyond the physical, though in the meantime it created a three-dimensional "painting" of seductive charm. Basically it reflected the contrasting principles which in the Taoist view understructured the universe itself, the active, masculine Yang and the passive, feminine Yin. This philosophical battle was represented by the juxtaposition of a rugged, upthrust form with a smoother, more recumbent one—two rocks, two trees, or two sections of the garden, perhaps a scaled-down landscape of hill and valley. Certain elements always had to be present: hills to represent the element of earth; rocks in certain shapes and numbers because they represented a variety of ethical and spiritual concepts; water because this seemingly passive element had the power to reshape the world. A pine tree meant graceful aging and strength against adversity. The willow spoke for tender friendship. Plum and peach trees stood for brotherly love.

237

With the spread of Buddhism, an even more ritualized symbolism infiltrated Oriental gardens, and it was taken many steps beyond the Chinese by the Japanese. Where Buddhism is practiced, such gardens still exist and thus they can become less mysterious—though never less complex—to the westerner willing to learn. A number of examples, like the Ryoanji garden mentioned in Chapter Eight, have been created or reproduced in this country. At a northerly point in Westchester County in New York State, on a hilltop from which one can look out over many miles of rolling country to the distant blue rise of the Berkshires, the Hammond Museum has built an elaborate landscape of Japanese gardens which demonstrates how the Orientals have ordered nature to serve and symbolize human aesthetic and spiritual needs. From springtime's flowering fruit trees to autumn's gentle-hued chrysanthemums, the growing and blossoming elements of the "stroll gardens" invite the visitor, as do the beautifully curving paths, set with small trees in perfect proportions. All is punctuated with water in such careful balance that the visitor absorbs serenity from the harmony around him. He need not try to remember that the stones he sees have names like the Guardian, the Stone of Worship, the Stone of the Two Deities. If he is at all receptive, his senses are soothed and his thoughts are released to soar, however briefly, out of petty preoccupations to the delights of meditation.

There is also here a Zen garden on the order of Ryoanji, in which sand and small stones and carefully chosen rocks compose an atmosphere that rigidly excludes all sensory distraction. To the student of Zen, the size, shape, and placement of these elements have endless meaning. But even the untutored westerner will find, if he gives himself to thought, that the very absence of minor sensation—the absence of color and scent—is so restful that his mind begins to function on an unaccustomed level. He can read whatever he likes into the stark rectangle; he can stare into it until he accomplishes a kind of autohypnosis. Sacheverell Sitwell saw in one Zen garden an enclosed space "as full of movement as Piccadilly Circus." But he went on to say that it was not human movement; that each time he looked at the stones they took on different meanings, and that while all the meanings were obscure they eventually suggested "an emptiness inhabited only by the primal forces." Any garden that can so free the mind and then provoke it into grappling with cosmic abstractions is surely entitled to be called a meditation garden, if not a major work of art.

Serious followers of oriental religions spend long years learning the techniques of meditation. In the Judeo-Christian tradition, it is chiefly men and women in religious vows who practice it as an active religious principle. The pattern was set in the sixth century when the Rule of St. Benedict prescribed a certain number of hours of meditation as one of the disciplines of the monastic day. When this meditation did not have to be solitary, it was frequently performed in the cloister garden—the enclosure which we have already seen functioning as botanical classroom, medicinal storehouse, and farm in miniature. We know from Strabo's diary that it was not only the bounty of these gardens but also their beauty that helped to direct a man's thoughts toward the splendor of his god and to reinforce his total dedication to his service.

238

Ornate aviary
(top) is focal
point of
Georgian
garden.
Bottom: Shelter
in modern
American
garden for
meditation.

Right: Monastery garden
in Tossa del Mar,
Spain. Below: Court of
monastery of
Saint-Guilhem restored at
The Cloisters, New York.
Opposite: Garden of
Greek nunnery (top).
Archway of monastery
garden at Granada.

*Right:
Architectural
detail such
as sundial may
lead mind
inward.
Opposite:
Garden provides
setting for
Indian poet's
17th-century
meditations.*

Such a medieval monastic environment has been created in The Cloisters, built on the heights of Fort Tryon Park in New York by the Metropolitan Museum of Art to house parts of its medieval collection. Even before the visitor reaches the building he is drawn into another time and another world. Around a hillside planted with fruit trees and evergreens—simulating the Mediterranean groves of cypress, olive, and palm which would not endure New York winters—paths spiral upward toward weathered gray stone towers protected by rampart walls. The walls enclose an approach drive, but this is paved, as are the entrance walks, with aged stone cobbles that evoke the streets of the old European towns where such monasteries sprang up. The very structure of The Cloisters is made up in part of actual sections of old monasteries brought from Spain and France, fitted together to convey the atmosphere both tangible and intangible in which the monks lived and worshiped.

The several gardens enclosed within the walls meticulously reproduce not only the simple, trim construction of the originals, but, insofar as they can be documented, the actual plantings. This was a difficult task; the only complete garden plan that exists—that of the ninth-century St. Gallen—gives little specific data on the plantings themselves. Many of the herbs, trees, and flowers in the various Cloister gardens are there as the result of research on the part of the curators, who painstakingly culled what they could from manuscripts and then searched paintings to identify the plants that medieval artists had seen in gardens of the time.

Pacing the narrow, straight paths, or sitting beneath the colonnades that surround the gardens, the visitor is granted a brief insight into the rewards of meditation in such surroundings. Even as a layman, he is likely to find here a peace of mind not easy to achieve in the world outside the walls.

Gardens conducive to meditation are still found attached to churches. The magnificent Bishop's Garden of the National Cathedral in Washington, D.C., offers a number of secluded spots. Outside St. Patrick's in Manhattan there is a small garden in which visitors are welcome to wander; in any town there are church gardens that invite a pause for contemplation. But there is no reason why a meditation garden cannot exist by itself, with no connection to a place of worship. What is important is that it provide a physical environment in which the fragmenting distractions of ordinary living can be pushed aside for a moment of contact with the fundamentals of a person's existence—with the values, the needs, the demands of his

Left: Small statue of happy child graces bed of flowers. Right: Roadside shrine in Austrian Alps has offering of fresh flowers.

relationship with himself and his world.

Perhaps the simplest of such flowering spots are those created high in the Alps —places so simple they can be called meditation "gardens" only because of the purpose they serve. In these mountains, it is the custom of the people to commemorate their loved ones by fixing a crudely painted picture—usually a Bible scene—to a stake in the ground, and to hang beneath it some container to hold the small flowers that grow at those heights. A little roof protects this shrine, and here, in a landscape of unsurpassed grandeur, the passerby may pause to pray or merely to think the thoughts he has no time for in the ordinary course of his day.

Anyone can create such a place for himself; he can do it in any corner of his own garden with a bench beneath a sheltering tree, or in a niche secluded by a hedge or flowering plants. As a focal point in this retreat, he can use whatever seems beautiful to him—an outstanding plant, a remarkable stone, a bit of oddly shaped wood, or a piece of sculpture. He must be shielded from intrusion, and draw pleasure from what is growing around him without being distracted by it; in such an atmosphere he can mend and purify his spirit.

There is little enough time for such moments, but the gardener who is conscious of them is able to create not only a more significant reward for his labors, but also a place for moments of silence and love in which he may be able to achieve by his union with nature a dimension far greater than his own.

Bibliography

Ancient History & Archeology

Bury, J. B., HISTORY OF GREECE, Revised ed.,
London, 1959

Childe, V. Gordon, NEW LIGHT ON THE MOST
ANCIENT EAST, London, 1952

Cottrell, Leonard (ed.), CONCISE ENCYCLOPEDIA OF
ARCHAEOLOGY, London, 1960

Kramer, S. N., HISTORY BEGINS AT SUMER,
London, 1958

Lange, K. and M. Hirmer, EGYPT, New York, 1957

Pritchard, James B., THE ANCIENT NEAR EAST,
Princeton, N. J., 1958

Rawlinson, George (trans.), THE HISTORY OF
HERODOTUS, New York, 1956

Rees, Ennis (trans.), THE ODYSSEY OF HOMER,
New York, 1960

Vaughan, Agnes Carr, THE HOUSE OF THE
DOUBLE AXE, Garden City, N.Y., 1959

Victoria and Albert Museum, INDIAN ART, London, 1948

Botany & Horticulture

Editors of Sunset Magazine and Sunset Books, HOW
TO GROW AND USE ANNUALS,
Menlo Park, Calif., 1965

——HOW TO GROW AND USE BULBS,
Menlo Park, Calif., 1962

Edmond, J. B., F. S. Senn, and F. S. Andrews,
FUNDAMENTALS OF HORTICULTURE,
New York, 1964

Fernald, M. L., GRAY'S MANUAL OF BOTANY,
8th ed., New York, 1950

Hutchins, Ross E., THE AMAZING SEEDS,
New York, 1965

——THIS IS A FLOWER, New York, 1963

——THIS IS A LEAF, New York, 1962

Smith, A. W., A GARDENER'S BOOK OF PLANT
NAMES, New York, 1963

Ferns

Foster, F. G., THE GARDENER'S FERN BOOK,
Princeton, N.J., 1964

Wherry, Edgar T., THE FERN GUIDE,
Garden City, N.Y., 1961

Garden Design

Brooklyn Botanic Garden, "Creative Ideas in Garden
Design," PLANTS AND GARDENS,
Vol. 21, No. 3, 1966

Clifford, Derek, A HISTORY OF GARDEN DESIGN,
London, 1966

Grant, John and Carol Grant, GARDEN DESIGN
ILLUSTRATED, Seattle, Wash., 1967

Gardens

Brooklyn Botanic Garden, "Gardens of Western Europe,"
PLANTS AND GARDENS, Vol. 16, No. 2, 1960

Bush-Brown, James and Louise Bush-Brown, AMERICA'S
GARDEN BOOK, New York, 1965

House and Garden, GARDEN GUIDE, New York, 1967

——COMPLETE BOOK OF GARDENING,
New York, 1955

Hyams, Edward, THE ENGLISH GARDEN,
New York, 1966

Masson, Georgina, ITALIAN GARDENS, New York, 1966

Page, Russell, THE EDUCATION OF A GARDENER,
New York, 1962

Reader's Digest, COMPLETE BOOK OF
THE GARDEN, Pleasantville, N.Y., 1966

Spencer, Edwin Rollin, JUST WEEDS, New York, 1940

Truex, Philip, THE CITY GARDENER, New York, 1963

General

Barnett, Jonathan, "Innovation and Symbolism on
42nd Street," ARCHITECTURAL RECORD,
Feb., 1968

Breasted, James H., THE DAWN OF CONSCIENCE,
New York, 1933

Moldenke, H. N. and A. L. Moldenke, PLANTS OF THE
BIBLE, New York, 1952

Sarton, George, A HISTORY OF SCIENCE,
Cambridge, Mass., 1952

Singer, E., E. D. Holmyard, and A. R. Hall, A HISTORY
OF TECHNOLOGY, Vol. 1, New York, 1957

Herbs & Vegetables

Brooklyn Botanic Garden, "Handbook on Herbs,"
PLANTS AND GARDENS, Vol. 14, No. 2, 1958

Clarkson, Rosetta, HERBS, THEIR CULTURE AND
USES, New York, 1966

Editors of Sunset Magazine and Sunset Books,
VEGETABLE GARDENING,
Menlo Park, Calif., 1966

Gerarde, John, THE HERBALL OR GENERAL
HISTORY OF PLANTS, London, 1636,
new ed. 1964

Herb Grower Magazine, HERBS FOR BEAUTY,
Falls Village, Conn., 1960

Krutch, Joseph Wood, HERBAL, New York, 1965

Leyel, C. F., CINQUEFOIL, London, 1957

Parkinson, John, PARADISI IN SOLE, PARADISUS
TERRESTRIS, London, 1629, fascimile, 1904

Sharon Audubon Center, HERBS IN THE GARDEN,
Falls Village, Conn.

History of Art

Bazin, Germain, A HISTORY OF ART, New York, 1959

Frankfort, Henri, THE ART AND ARCHITECTURE
OF THE ANCIENT ORIENT, Baltimore, Md., 1954

Grabar, André and Carl Nordenfalk, EARLY
MEDIEVAL PAINTING, New York, 1957

Maiuri, Amedeo, ROMAN PAINTING, New York, 1953

Metropolitan Museum of Art, "Mesopotamian
Manuscripts," BULLETIN, May, 1950

Newton, Eric, EUROPEAN PAINTING AND
SCULPTURE, Middlesex, England, 1941

Philadelphia Museum, "A World of Flowers,"
BULLETIN, Spring, 1963

History of Plants & Gardens

Berrall, Julia S., THE GARDEN, New York, 1966

Eifert, Virginia S., TALL TREES AND FAR
HORIZONS, New York, 1965

Fairbrother, Nan, "Gardens Since Eden," HORIZON,
New York, May, 1959

————MEN AND GARDENS, New York, 1956

Hedrick, U. P., A HISTORY OF AMERICAN
HORTICULTURE TO 1860, New York, 1950

Herbst, Josephine, NEW GREEN WORLD,
New York, 1954

Krutch, Joseph Wood, THE GARDENER'S WORLD,
New York, 1959

Metropolitan Museum of Art, GARDENS AS
ILLUSTRATED IN PRINTS, New York, 1949

Taylor, R. L., PLANTS OF COLONIAL DAYS,
Williamsburg, Va., 1952

Tergit, Gabrielle, FLOWERS THROUGH THE AGES,
London, 1961

Wright, Richardson, THE STORY OF GARDENING,
New York, 1963

Indoor Gardens

Budlong, Ware, INDOOR GARDENS, New York, 1967

Cathey, Henry, INDOOR GARDEN FOR DECORATIVE
PLANTS, Washington, D. C., 1965

Home and Garden Bulletin #82, SELECTING AND
GROWING HOUSE PLANTS,
Washington, D. C., June, 1962

Lee, Elsie, AT HOME WITH PLANTS, New York, 1966

Mythology & Folklore

Hollingsworth, Buckner, FLOWER CHRONICLES,
New Brunswick, N.J., 1958

Lehner, Ernst and Johanna Lehner, FOLKLORE AND
SYMBOLISM OF FLOWERS, PLANTS,
AND TREES, New York, 1960

Nature

Borland, Hal, SUNDIAL OF THE SEASONS,
Philadelphia, 1964

Brooklyn Botanic Garden, "Conservation for Every Man,"
PLANTS AND GARDENS, Vol. 18, No. 2, 1962

Hersey, Jean, A SENSE OF SEASONS, New York, 1964

Milne, Lorus and Margery Milne, PATTERNS
OF SURVIVAL, Englewood Cliffs, N. J., 1967

Thoreau, Henry David, WALDEN, New York, 1950

Plants: Dangers & Uses of

Creekmore, Hubert, DAFFODILS ARE DANGEROUS,
New York, 1966

Genders, Roy, PERFUME IN THE GARDEN,
London, 1955

Gibbons, Euell, STALKING THE WILD ASPARAGUS,
New York, 1962

Rock, Water, & Alpine Plants

Foster, H. Lincoln, ROCK GARDENING, Boston, 1958

Green, C. and M. G. Potts, THE SALTY THUMB,
Montauk, N.Y., 1967

Hills, Lawrence D., ALPINE GARDENING,
London, 1955

Mercer, F. A. and Roy Hay (eds.), ROCK WALL
AND WATER, London (n.d.)

Trees & Shrubs

Faust, Joan Lee (ed.), THE NEW YORK TIMES
BOOK OF TREES AND SHRUBS, New York, 1964

Hutchins, Ross E., THIS IS A TREE, New York, 1964

Petrides, George A., A FIELD GUIDE TO TREES
AND SHRUBS, Boston, 1958

Platt, Rutherford, THE GREAT AMERICAN FOREST,
Englewood Cliffs, N. J., 1965

Wildflowers

Birdseye, C. and E. G. Birdseye, GROWING
WOODLAND PLANTS, New York, 1951

Craighead J., F. C. Craighead, and R. J. Davis, FIELD
GUIDE TO ROCKY MOUNTAIN
WILDFLOWERS, Boston, 1963

Dietz, Marjorie J., FAVORITE WILD FLOWERS,
Garden City, N.Y., 1965

Howard, Richard A., FLOWERS OF STAR ISLAND,
ISLES OF SHOALS, Cambridge, Mass., 1968

Lemmon, R. S and C. C. Johnson, WILDFLOWERS OF
NORTH AMERICA, Garden City, N.Y., 1961

Peterson, R. T. and M. McKenny, A FIELD GUIDE
TO WILDFLOWERS, Boston, 1968

Rickett, H. W., THE NEW FIELD BOOK OF
AMERICAN WILD FLOWERS, New York, 1963

Steffek, E. F., WILD FLOWERS AND HOW TO
GROW THEM, New York, 1963

von Miklos, Josephine, WILDFLOWERS IN
YOUR HOUSE, Garden City, N.Y., 1968

Wherry, Edgar T., WILD FLOWER GUIDE,
New York, 1948

Picture Credits

All pictures are by Josephine von Miklos except the following:
MM—The Metropolitan Museum of Art
BM—By Courtesy of the Trustees of the British Museum
CW—Colonial Williamsburg Photograph
JP—John Parkinson, "Paradisi in Sole, Paradisus Terrestris," London, 1629

CHAPTER ONE
10-11: BM. 12: MM, Museum Excavations, 1919-1920, Rogers Fund. 15: MM. 16 (top): MM, gift of J. Pierpont Morgan, 1917; (bottom): MM, Museum Excavations, 1922-1923, Rogers Fund. 17: BM. 18 (top): Israel Information Services, N.Y.; (bottom, left): MM, Rogers Fund; (bottom right): MM, Rogers Fund. 20: Biblioteca Apostolica, Vatican. 22: MM, gift of J. Pierpont Morgan, 1917. 23: Philadelphia Museum of Art. 24: Städelsches Kunstinstitut, Frankfurt, Germany. 25: BM. 26 (top and lower left): MM, Harris Brisbane Dick Fund; (lower right): Courtesy of the Trustees of the Victoria and Albert Museum.

CHAPTER TWO
28-29: Harry T. Peters Collection, Museum of the City of New York. 32: Benson Murray. 33: Elizabeth Burris-Meyer. 34-35: MM, Harris Brisbane Dick Fund. 36 (top): Muriel Hinerfeld; (below): U.S. Department of the Interior. 37: CW.

CHAPTER THREE
40-41: Gene Federico. 43: John G. Johnson Collection, Philadelphia. 45 (top): Stephen Ash. 47 (top left): U.S. Department of Agriculture; (top right): Chicago Sun-Times; (middle right): John Benson; (bottom): Kunsthistorisches Museum, Vienna. 52 (both): Kunsthistorisches Museum, Vienna. 57: John Benson.

CHAPTER FOUR
58-59: Roy Goldfinger. 61 (top): Roy Goldfinger; (bottom left): Richard Goldfinger. 62 (top two): Ross E. Hutchins, Mississippi State College; (bottom): Miroslav Schreiber, Prague. 64 (1): Margaret Freisner; (2): Harry Brevoort; (3): Werner Schulz; (4): Roy Goldfinger. 65: Patrimoine Des Musees Royaux Des Beaux-Arts, Brussels. 67: Ross E. Hutchins.

CHAPTER FIVE
71: Uffizi Gallery. 76: JP. 78: Mrs. Grover E. Bode (Yellow Lady's-Slippers). 81: The Pierpont Morgan Library. 85: Abby Aldrich Rockefeller Folk Art Collection, Williamsburg. 91 (top left): Richard Goldfinger.

CHAPTER SIX
97: JP. 98: Albert Squillace (Daisy).

CHAPTER SEVEN
114-115: MM, Harris Brisbane Dick Fund. 119: CW. 122-123 (left): Garden designed by Frede Stege; (center): CW. 125 (top left): Garden designed by Frede Stege; (bottom): CW. 127 (top right & bottom): Albert Squillace. 133: CW. 134-135: (top center): Garden designed by the Hammond Museum, North Salem, N.Y. 134 (bottom right): Garden designed and photographed by James Fanning; (bottom left): Garden designed by Charles Middeleer.

CHAPTER EIGHT
142, 143, 145, & 146: Mrs. Grover H. Bode. 149 (left): JP. 151: The Rare Book Department of the Free Library of Philadelphia. 152-153 (top left & right): John P. Merriam. 157 (bottom): Muriel Hinerfeld. 161 (top left): Roy Goldfinger.

CHAPTER NINE
164-165: Designed by Natalie Hammond 'for the Hammond Museum. 175 (bottom): Mrs. Grover H. Bode. 176: Rheinisches Landesmuseum, Bonn, W. Germany.

CHAPTER TEN
180: The Pierpont Morgan Library. 183: JP. 186-187: MM, Whittelsey Fund. 188 (left): Albertina, Vienna. 190: BM. 193: CW. 196-197: JP. 198-199: Garden designed by Helen Whitman, Tool Shed Nursery, North Salem, N.Y.

CHAPTER ELEVEN
202-203: Muriel Hinerfeld. 205 (top): Theodora Hausman; (bottom): Helen Federico. 206 (top): Ralph Bailey. 207: Albert Squillace. 208-209: All from the U.S. Department of the Interior. 210: Kunsthistorisches Museum, Vienna. 212: Columbia Broadcasting System. 213 (top): The Rachel McMasters Miller Hunt Botanical Library, Pittsburgh; (bottom): Ford Foundation. 214 (top): MM, Rogers Fund; (bottom): The Rouse Company, Columbia, Maryland.

CHAPTER TWELVE
216-217: Old Sturbridge Village, Mass. 219: Abby Aldrich Rockefeller Folk Art Collection, Williamsburg. 220: Grown by Frances Merriam. 222: Courtesy of Detroit Institute of Art. 223: Uffizi Gallery. 226-227: House and gardens designed by Jean Hersey. 230: Window box designed by Elizabeth Burris-Meyer.

CHAPTER THIRTEEN
232-233: Washington Cathedral, Washington, D.C. 235: MM, Harris Brisbane Dick Fund. 236-237: Hammond Museum, North Salem, N.Y. 239 (top): MM, Harris Brisbane Dick Fund; (bottom): Ralph Bailey. 240-241 (top left & lower right): Theodora Hausman; (bottom): MM, Cloisters Collection. 242: Washington Cathedral, Washington, D.C. 243: Museum of Fine Arts, Boston.

Index *Picture references in italics*

Acanthus, 21
Addison, Joseph, 34
African violet, 218, 229
Agueweed, see Boneset
Akkadian gardening, 14
Alberti, Leon Battista, 30
Alexanders, golden, *107*, 108
Alkanet, 184
Alpine gardens, 146, 155-156
Alpine rose, 156
Alps, 244
American gardens, 36-39, *115*, 119, 123, 133, 135, 232-233, 236, 239, 240-241
Anemone, 32, 36, *75*, 80
Angelica, *189*
Anise, 192
Anthers, 63
Apple tree, 46, *86*
Aquatic plants, 173
Arbutus, trailing, 70, *78*, 83, 159
Arrowhead, 173
Artificial lighting, *220*, 222-223
Ashurbanipal, 14-15
Assyrian gardening, 14-16
Aster, 36, 52
    New England, *103*, 105
Augustus, Tomb of, 21
Austen, Jane, 35
Azalea, 52, 73, *131*, 229
    dwarf, *152*, 156
    in rock garden, *144*
    wild, *72*

Babylonian gardening, 14-16
Bachelor's button, 96
Bacon, Francis, 144
Baneberry, *74*, 77
Barberry family, 77
Bartram, John and William, 38
Basket-of-gold, *144*
Beach plums, 168, 169
Beans, 196
"Bedded-out" style, 35, 129, 132
Bee balm, *78*, 83
Beet, 198
Begonia, 38, 66
Bellwort, *78*, 80
Belvedere Palace Garden (Vienna), *152*
Bergamot, *79*, 83
Betony, *78*, 81, 182
Bindweed, 53, *96*, *106*, 108
Binomial nomenclature, 52
Birches, *172*
Black snakeroot, *74*
Black-eyed Susan, 36, *99*, 101, *161*
Bladder campion, *106*, 108

Bleeding heart, Wild, *78*, 83
Blenheim Gardens, 34
Bloodroot, *74*, 77
Blue lobelia, *78*, 83, *161*
Blue spruce, *86*
Blue vervain, 105
Bluebells, *161*
Blue-curls, 105
Blue-eyed grass, *103*, 105
Bluets, *103*, 104-105
Bo tree, 14
Bog gardens, 173, 177
Boneset, *98*, 101
Bonsai gardens, 156
Borghese Gardens, 30
Boston Common, 204
Botanical gardens
    Claremont, California, 146
    Dutch, 31
    first in U.S., 30, 38
Botany, foundations of, 20
Bottle gentian, 111
Bouncing Bet, *106*, 108
Boxwood, *123*
Broccoli, 197
Brooklyn Botanical Garden, 146
Browallia, *225*
Brown, Lancelot, 34, 35
Buddhism, 234, 238
Bull thistle, *96*
Bunchberry, *93*, 111
Burdock, *107*, 110
Burnet, 186
Buttercup, 60, 66, *99*, 101
    family, 77, 80, 83
Butterfly weed, *99*, 104

Cabbage, 193, *195*
Cacti, *228*, 229
Calyx, 63
Camellias, 229
Camomile, 184
Campion, 53, *106*, 108
Canada anemone, *75*
Canada Mayflower, *75*, 77
Carboniferous era, 42
Cardinal flower, 70, 111, 137, *161*, 173, 177
Carnation, 37
Catesby, Mark, 38
Cauliflower, *195*, 197
Causes of Plants (Theophrastus), 20
Celandine, *48*
Central Park (N.Y.), 39, 210
Cereus, 52
Cheeses, *106*, 110

Chicory, 53, 96
Chinese gardens, 237, 238
Chives, 191
Christmas fern, *90*, *91*, 93
Christmas-cactus, *228*
Chrysanthemum, 52, *117*
Cinnamon fern, 93
City gardens, 39, *206*, *207*
Clayton, John, 38
Clematis, *131*
Clianthus, 13
Climbing rose, *116*
Clintonia, 81
Cloister gardens, 238, 242
Cloisters, The (N.Y.), *240*, 242
Cobbett, William, 35
Cohosh, see Baneberry
Colchicum, 182
Collinson, Peter, 38, 92
Coltsfoot, *48*
Columbia, Maryland, *215*
Columbine, 72, 73
    leaves, *185*
Conifers, first appearance, 42
Conservation, 33
    and wildflower gardens, 159, 162
Coreopsis, *63*, *161*
Cornflower, 66, 96
Corolla, 63
Crane's-bill, see Wild geranium
Cresses, 173
Cretaceous era, 46
Crowfoot family, 77
Crown vetch, *102*, 104
Cucumber, 66, 196
Culinary herbs, 186-192
Culpeper, 110, 192
Cyclamen, *227*, 228

Daisy, 66, *98*
    oxeye, 96, 100
Dandelion, 96, *107*, 136
Day lily, 101
Day-neutral plants, 52
De re aedificatoria (Alberti), 30
Delphinium, *120*, 186
Deptford pink, 104
Devil's-paintbrush, *107*
Digitalis, 184, *189*
Dioscorides, *19*
Dogbane, *109*, 111
Dogwood, 52, *87*, *89*, 128
    leaf, *64*
Donck, Adrian van der, 36, 37
Downing, A. J., 38-39
Dumbarton Oaks, 36, 39, *215*

Dutch gardens, 31-32
Dutchman's-breeches, *74*, 77, 159
Dwarfs
    azalea, *152*
    Bonsai, 156
Dyes, herbal, 184

Edelweiss, *152*, 156
Eel grass, 166
Eggplant, 197
Eglantine, 32, 33
Egyptian Book of the Dead, 234
Egyptian gardens, *12*, *15*, 16-19
Egyptian lotus, 169, *171*
English Garden, The (Cobbett), 35
English gardens, 25, 27, 32-36
Epicurus, 19-20
Erosion, preventives, 168
Estate gardens, 33, 34, 39
Euphorbia, *72*, *185*
Evelyn, John, 33
Evening primrose, 50, 52
Everglade orchid, *63*

Fences, 118, 121, *123*
Fenugreek, 96
Fern gardens, *161*, 162, 163
Ferns, 49, *64*, 90, *91*, *92*, 93
    indoors, 229, 231
    types, 162
Fertilizers, early, 38
Fevergrass, see Blue-eyed grass
Fireweed, *103*, 104
Flora Virginica (Gronovius), 38
Floral clock, 53
Floral symbolism, 234
Florentine gardens, 30
Flowering trees, 128-129
Flowers
    first appearance, 42, 60
    parts, 63, 66
    perfect and imperfect, 66
Ford Foundation building, *213*
Forget-me-not, 85
Forsythia, 38, 129
Foxglove, 184, *189*
French gardens, 30-31
Fringed gentian, *103*, 111
Fumitory family, 77

Garden design, 114-137
    Japanese, *150*, 238
"Gardenesque" style, 39
Gardenia (shrub), 229
Gardening, origins and history, 12-27,
    30-39

Gentian, 66, 156, 177
    Bottle, 111
    Fringed, *103*, 111
Geraniums
    indoor, 227, 229
    wild, *79*, 84
Gerard, John, 32, 100
Giant purple loosestrife, *109*, 111
Gillyflower, 104
Ginger, wild, 84
Golden alexanders, *107*, 108
Goldenrod, mountain, 156
Goldthread, 77, *154*
Grass of Parnassus, *98*, 100
Gray, Asa, 96
Greek gardens, 19-21
Greek Valerian, see Jacob's-Ladder
Greenhouses, *222*, 225, *226*
Gronovius, John F., 38
Ground cherry, *107*
Ground covers, 128
Groundsel, *99*, 101

Hadrian, Tomb of, 21
Hamilton, William, 88
Hammond Museum, *237*, 238
Hanging Gardens of Babylon, 16
Hardhack, 111
Harebell, *50*
Hatfield House, 33
Hawkweed, 108, 110
Hawthorn, *131*
Heal-all, *109*, 110
Heath family, 83
Heather, *156*, *158*
Hedge bindweed, 108
Heliocereus, *228*
Heliotrope, *189*
Hemlock, 88
"Hens-and-chickens," 155
Hepatica, *78*, 83, 159
Herb, definition, 129, 181
Herb gardens, 182-192
    circular, 192, 200
Herbal medicine, 25, 27, 32, 100-105,
    110, 111, 182-184
Herball (Gerard), 32, 100
Herbariums, monastery, 23
Hermaphroditic flowers, 66
Hibiscus, 52
Hickory, *87*
History of Plants (Theophrastus), 20
Holly, *126*
Hollyhocks, 36, 37
Hongo, 181
Horsemint, see Bergamot

Horsetail, *91*, 93
Hothouses, first, 21
House plants, 218-231
Huckleberry, 168
Humidity, in indoor gardening, 223
Humus, 56
Hyacinth, 60
Hyde Park (London), 207

Ilex, 129
Indian blanket, *64*
Indian cucumber root, 81
Indian paint, see Bloodroot
Indian turnip, see Jack-in-the-pulpit
Indoor gardens, 217-231
Insect-pollinated flowers, 67
Interrupted fern, *92*, 93
Iris, *72*, 76, *116*, *151*, 177
    in rock garden, *147*
    in seaside gardens, 169
Irisette, see Blue-eyed grass
Irish moss, 166
Ironweed, *103*, 105
Italian gardens, 30
Ivy, 128

Jack-in-the-pulpit, *79*, 84
Jacob's-ladder, 83
Japanese gardens, 146, 150, 238
Jefferson, Thomas, 37-38
Jekyll, Gertrude, 132
Jewelweed, *50*
Jimson weed, 184
Joe-pye weed, *102*, 105
Josselyn, John, 37

Kalanchoe, *228*
Kalm, Peter, 92
Kensington Gardens, 34
Kent, William, 34
Kew Gardens, 34, 35, 237
Kidney vetch, *152*

Lady fern, *90*
Lady's-slipper, *63*, *78*
Lady's-thumb, 110
Landscape gardening
    American, 38-39
    English, 34-36
    Florentine, 30
Larkspur, 186
Laurel, 21
Lavender, 191
Lawns, *123*
LeBlond, Alexandre, 31
L'Ecluse, Charles, 31

250

Leech Book of Bald, 25
Leek, *194*
L'Enfant, Pierre, 215
Le Nôtre, André, 30-32
Lettuce, 52, 192, 193
Lichens, 53
Light
    artificial, 222-223
    plant requirements, 49-53
Lilac, 36, 129, *131*
Lilies, 73, 76, 169, 173
    Christian symbolism, 25
    water, 53, 66, *82, 85, 166,
    168, 169, 170, 173*
    see also individual species
Lily family, 77, 80-81
Lily-of-the-valley, 80
Linnaeus, Carolus, 52-53
Live oak, *88*
Liverwort, see Hepatica
Lobelia, *78*, 83, *161*
London parks, 215
Long-day plants, 52
Longwood Gardens, *36*, 39
Loosestrife, Giant purple, *109*, 111
Lotus, 85, *171*
Lupine, *102, 105*

Madder, 184
Madonna lily, *23, 72, 76*
Magnolia, 60, 128
Maiden Pink, *102, 104*
Maidenhair fern, *92, 93*
Maize, 196
Mallow
    Common, 60, 110
    Musk, *102, 104*
Mandrake, 75, 77, *81, 181, 186*
Maple, *86, 88, 128,* 168
    blossoms, *88*
    Red, 33
    serpentine, *127*
Marguerite, 100
Marigold, 53, *82, 88,* 192
Mariposa lily, *116*
Marjoram, 191
Mauve, 110
May apple, *75, 77*
Mayflower, Canada, *75, 77*
Maypole, origin, 13
Meadow plants, see Wildflowers
Meadow rue, *98,* 101
Meadowsweet, *109,* 111
Medicinal plants, see Herbal medicine
Medieval gardening, 23-27
Metropolitan Museum of Art, 242

Michaelmas daisy, 33
Milkweed, *64, 109,* 110
Mint, 192
Mint family, 83
Monastery gardens, 23-27, *234, 240*
Monticello (Jefferson's estate), 37-38
Morning-glory, 53, *175*
"Mosaic culture," 35
Moscow parks, 215
Mount Vernon (Washington's estate), 37
Mountain laurel, *87, 92*
Mulches, *55*
    seaside gardens, 169
Musk mallow, *102, 104*

National Cathedral (Washington, D.C.),
    234, 242
National forests, 207
Neanderthal man, 234
Near Eastern gardening, 14-16
Nebuchadnezzar, 16
Norway maple, *88*

Oak, 21, 66, *89,* 127
Olmsted, Frederick Law, 39, 210
Orchid family, 81
Orchids, *63*
Oregano, 191
Oriental gardens, 23, 146, 150, 237, 238
Ostrich fern, 93
Ovary, 63
Oxeye daisy, 96, 100

Paleobotany, 42, 46
Paley Park, 204, *213*
Paradisi in Sole, Paradisus Terrestris
    (Parkinson), 32, *76, 104, 149, 183*
Parkinson, John, 32, 37, 104
Parks, origin, 204, 207
    see also Public gardens
Paths, see Walks and paths
Peace rose, *116*
Peach tree, 237
Peas, *197*
Peat moss, 169
Pepper, 197
Perennials, 132, 138-141
    border, 136
"Perfect" flowers, 66
Persian gardens, 23
Petals, 63-64
Peter the Great, 33
Petunia, 38, 60
Phlox, 36, *79*
Photoperiod, 52
Photosynthesis, 49

"Physick" gardens, 30, 32
Pickerelweed, *82, 85, 173, 177*
Pine, 20, *86, 88,* 237
Pink lady's-slipper, *78*
Pinks, 102, 104, *117,* 149
    in rock garden, *147*
Pinxter, *72, 73*
Pistil, 63
Pitcher plant, *93,* 177
Plantain, *64*
Plants, evolution of, 42, 46
Pleurisy root, 104
Plum tree, 237
Poinsettia, 221
Pollination, 66-67
Polo, Marco, 237
Pompeian gardens, 21
Pond lily, *82, 85,* 173
Poppy, 17, 19, *99, 120, 152*
Poppy family, 77
Potpourri, 186
Primrose, *50, 120,* 228
    indoors, *220*
Prunella, *161*
Public gardens and parks, 203-215
    American, 39
    English, 33
    Roman, 21
Purple loosestrife, *109,* 111
Pyxies, *154*

Quaker-lady, see Bluets
Queen Anne's lace, 96, *106,* 108, *168,* 198

Radish, 181
Ragwort, see Groundsel
Rattlesnake plantain, *51*
Rattlesnake root, *78*
Red pine, *86*
Red trillium, *78*
Redwoods, 14
Regeneration myths, 13-14
Renaissance gardens, 30
Reproduction, plant, 42, *61, 63, 64,
    66,* 60-67
Rhododendron, 129
Roan mountain thorn, *126*
Rock garden, *144, 147,* 144-155, *158*
    waterside, 173
Rocks, choice, for gardens, 150-151
Rockweed, 166
Roman gardens, 21-23, *213*
Root plants, 198
Rose geranium, *185*
Rose of Sharon, 129, *131,* 169
Rosemary, 191

Roses, *61*, 66, *99*, *116*, *117*, *175*
   in antiquity, 17, 21
   Christian symbolism, 25
   in history, 27, 96, 100
   medical and culinary uses, 100
   in seaside gardens, 169
   see also individual species
Rue, *98*, 101
Ryoanji Temple garden, 146, 238

Sage, 191
Saihoji Temple garden, 146
St. Benedict, 23, 238
St. Gallen, 23-24, 242
St. Patrick's Cathedral (N.Y.), 242
Salad, origin of, 184
Salad garden, *198*
Salt hay, 169
Sarsaparilla, *48*
Sassafras, 88
Savory, 186
Saxifrage, 159
Scotch broom, *109*, 111
Scouring rush, *91*
Scree, 151, 155
Seaside gardens, 166-169, *174*
Sedums, 150, 169
Seeds
   first appearance, 42
   reproduction, 60, 63, 66
Selfheal, see Heal-all
Self-pollination, 66
Senna, 184, *185*
Sennacherib, 14
Serpentine maple, *127*
Shadbush, 89
Shallot, 191
Short-day plants, 52
Shrines, roadside, 244
Sitwell, Sacheverell, 238
Skullcap, *50*
Skunk cabbage, *48*, 84
Snakeroot, black, *74*
Snapdragon family, 80, 81
Snow-on-the-mountain, *147*
Soapwort, see Bouncing Bet
Soil, 53, *55*, 56
Solomon's-seal, *74*, 77
Spiderwort, 108
Spindle tree, *51*
Spores, 42, 60
Spring beauty, *48*
Spruce, *86*
Stamens, 63
Star thistle, 96
Stigma, 63

Stockholm parks, 215
Stone walls, as gardens, 155
Strabo, Walafrid, 16, 24-25, 238
String beans, 196
Strybing Arboretum, 146
Sumerian gardening, 14
Sunflower, 36, 52, 63, *117*
Swamp-candles, *50*
Sylva (Evelyn), 33

Taoism, 234, 237
Tarragon, 191
Temperature, influence on plants, 53
Terraces, 121, *128*
Theophrastus, 20
Thistle, *96*, 111
Thoreau, Henry David, 204
Thorn-apple, *96*
Thoroughwort, see Joe-pye weed
Thyme, 191
Tiglath-pileser, 14
Tobacco, *96*
Topiary gardening, 21, 30, 34
Tradescant, John, 32-33, 108
Trailing arbutus, 70, *78*, 83, 159
Transplanting, trees, 88
Tree of Life, 14
Trees
   longevity, 14
   in mythology, 20-21
   in seaside gardens, 168
   transplanting, 88
   worship, 13-14
   see also individual species
Trees, bushes, and shrubs, *86-87*, 88-89,
   89, 92
   flowering, 128-129
   selection for garden, 124, 128-129
Trianon, Le Petit, *33*, 207
Trillium, *74*, *78*, 80
Trinity Church (N.Y.), 234
Trout lilies, 162
Tuileries Gardens, 31
Tulip, 32, 60, 66, *119*, *120*
   pistils and stamen, *64*
Tulip tree, *86*, 89, 128, 168
Turtlehead, *75*, 80

Valerian, 182
Vaux, Calvert, 39, 210
Vegetable, definition, 181
Vegetable garden, 192-198
   circular, 192, *201*
Vegetative reproduction, 60
Versailles, Palace of, 30
Vervain, *102*, 105

Vetch, 102, 104, *152*
Villa d'Este, 30
Violets, 72, *75*, 80, *102*, 105
   see also African violet
Viper's bugloss, 110
Virginia creeper, *51*

Walks and paths, 118, 121, *123*, *135*,
   136, 155
Washington, George, 37
Washington parks, *208*, 215
Water, plant dependence on, 46
Water lilies, 53, 66, *82*, 85, *166*,
   168, 169, *170*, 173
Weeds
   definition, 96
   identification, 108, 110-111
White campion, 108
White pine, *86*, 88
White poplar, see Tulip tree
White trillium, *74*
White violet, *75*
Wigela, 52, 129
Wildflower gardens, 156-162
Wildflowers, 70-93, 96-111
   identification, 77, 80, 81, 83-85,
      100-101, 104-105, 108, 110-111
   illustrations, *72*, *74-75*, *78-79*, *82*, *93*,
      98-99, *102-103*, *106-107*, *109*
   see also individual species
Williamsburg, Virginia, *36*, *119*, *133*
Willow, *171*, 237
Windflower, see Wood anemone
Wind-pollinated flowers, 67
Winged spindle tree, *51*
Wintergreen, spotted, *51*
Winterthur Gardens, 39
Wisteria, 38
Witch hazel, *87*, 92
Woad, 184
Wood anemone, *75*, 80
Wood betony, *78*, 81
Woodbine, *51*
Woodland violet, *72*

Yang principle, 237
Yarrow, 96, *98*
Yellow lady's-slipper, *78*, 81
Yellow peace rose, *116*
Yellow rocket, *50*
Yin principle, 237
Yucca, *98*

Zen gardens, *237*, 238
Zinnias, 198
Zucchini, *194*